THE DUCKS

A story of our time

Len Horridge

Len Horridge

Len Horridge was born in England and stayed there. Which is where he still lives. He learned to write at school and, many years later, learned how to read. He has never looked back without falling over. As well as writing, he does many things, some of which he wants to do, drinks tea and eats the occasional biscuit which is better than eating an occasional table. He has met many famous people but is not famous himself. His favourite film of all time is "Duck Soup".

42

Also by Len Horridge

The Unbreakable Strength of Stupidity
A collection of short stories

T&D: Managing Change In A Ship Of Fools
A sitcom, unperformed

Detention
Screenplay, un-filmed

Too Short
Another collection of short stories

Cinderella and the Forty Jokes
A pantomime

Wogan & Me
Autobiography

2055: the seven wonders
A book

An assumed excerpt from the lost parts of "The Life and Prophecies of Ursula Sontheil" (better known as Mother Shipton first published about 1502 or just after three, European Summer Time).

"And from the raining skies shall come
Downed creatures, block the sun
Will kill and maim and quack and laugh
To see the death of a giraffe
From north to south their hordes descend
To witness Britain's bloody end
Unless a one-armed man shall come
To take away the clouds from sun
With others he can save the isle
It may just even raise a smile
As humans die and bills are bloodied
Their task to save should not be hurried
But meet at abbey's endless mouth
Saving the north and saving the south
Before another threat should roar
Beware the yelping…"

And this is where the document tails off.
It has never been found.

THE DUCKS

Based on a myth and an untrue story

Len Horridge

Len Horridge

"Behold the duck.
It does not cluck.
A cluck it lacks.
It quacks."
Ogden Nash

"If you're going to tell a joke involving an animal, make it a duck."
Psychologist Richard Wiseman

"When in doubt, duck."
Malcolm Forbes

"If it walks like a duck, quacks like a duck, looks like a duck, it must be a duck."
Proverb

"This grown up man, with pluck and luck, is hoping to outwit a duck."
Ogden Nash

"Lambs are scarier... otherwise it would have been called Silence Of The Ducks!"
Chandler, Friends

"Ducks? Don't talk to me about ducks."
Un-attributed

This book is dedicated to me and Siri Hustvedt.

FOREWORD

There are many prophecies that abound in this world of ours, today and in our past. Most are over-looked as heresy, myth and delusion but some are taken as potential truth and psychic insight into our future and our destiny.

It is true that these echoing voices of turbulent times and terrible fortunes are listened to most in times of great change and seismic movement. Our own time is one such time.

It was foretold, many, many years ago by a common uneducated woman, born of unmarried parents and scorned by her local community for fear of her looks and her predictions, not to mention her bad breath, that the country of her birth would, when the cliffs of finance came crashing into the sea, fall foul of a strange and unforeseen danger, lurking within our midst.

She told of the seemingly friendly beasts who would use the time of unforeseen turmoil to finally wreak their own vengeance on those who had fed and watered them for many years, taking their chance to turn this world on its head and to bring it to the brink of annihilation and their own victory.

"They shall come, with look of down
To take the islands as their own.
To kill and slaughter all who dare
Stand in their way, with fearful glare.
When fools bring down the wheels of gold
Your mortgaged lives have all been sold.
The race is running out of luck..
You won't believe it of a duck."

But she also foretold of our potential saviours, a triumvirate of hapless souls, thrown together to unwittingly be the heroes. The one-armed man, the female of the plastic legs and the man oblivious to all.

13

"And those three shall stand
All in one place.
A generation lost in space.
With bread and powder in their hands
To thwart the evil beings' plans.
A holy place
A mighty bang
For peace at last throughout the land.
But will they heed this terrible warning?
Or is this mankind's final dawning?"

It was a warning, distinct and chilling yet ignored, save for the part that Don McLean put into American Pie.

It was a warning of the end of the world.

Tucked away in a church in North Yorkshire.

Where nobody seemed to pay any attention.

Until now.

When nature called...and the mysterious power of prophecy came home to the collection of lands we used to know as Britain.

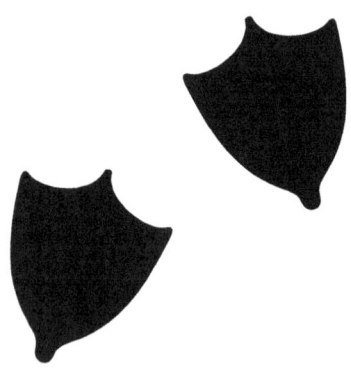

PROLOGUE

The late evening breeze glided wistfully down the banks of the river, gently rippling the waters, as the last of the visitors ambled along in the warm evening air of a cloudless night. The huge orange floodlights of the Abbey crackled into life, shedding unnatural light onto the edifice that pushed into the hills of the surrounding countryside.

In the river, amongst the large, poker like reeds that skirted it at almost every point, two mallards lurked, unnoticed, in the gathering gloom. In tandem, like mirror images, they glided purposefully, seemingly smiling, moving their heads only momentarily to carefully check their surroundings, ignoring the swooping bats that had come out to start their early evening feast of flies and moths.

They stopped. Not a noise was heard, save for that of a small boy, laughing impishly as he ran towards the bank of the river.

The ducks exchanged a glance, their eyes, dark and merciless, flashing in the glare of the arc-lights.

"Johnny, come back, Johnny," pleaded a mother's voice from the trees on the surrounding hills as she ran down towards the river.

The boy stopped, feet from the bank. The ducks could see his plump feet and thighs, bare toes moving around in his sandals. They quacked, quietly, in anticipation, saliva rising in their beaks.

The boy stopped and looked around.

The ducks held their breath and held a cold stare at their quarry.

The boy swiveled round then started again towards the bank, laughing at the game with his mother.

"Johnny!" she shouted this time, no longer exasperated, this time a hint of malice in her exhausted voice. She'd had a hard time with Johnny. He was an only child, born out of wedlock, as the quaint phrase goes, his father being one of two, or three, maybe four, men who had drifted around and in and out of her life. She could have had an abortion but didn't realize she was pregnant until her waters broke and she reasoned that it was too late then. She didn't want to be a mother, she just wanted to be herself, a fat slag who slept around. Of course, this didn't mean that she wasn't a bad mother, she just preferred shopping, that's all. And sleeping around. And drinking, obviously, and going out with her friends, which was all the more difficult since Johnny had come along. But she didn't despise him. Just found him occasionally irritating.

"Johnny, come back, Johnny," she pleaded again.

The boy stopped once again. Just a foot short of the bank, the toes twiddled and fidgeted tantalisingly close to the beaks of the ducks hidden in the reeds.

"Just wanna see the 'ickle ducks, Ma," he shouted back in annoyance, "like 'ickle ducks."

"There ain't no more ducks, they're all in bed," came his mother's reply from the gathering gloom. "And if you don't come here..."

"What, Ma, will you kill me?" he retorted with a sarcasm that belied his young years.

"I'll do worse than that..." she started, then stopped as she heard a huge splash of water.

"Aaargh!" she exploded. "If you're in that water you're in for it my lad, I'll tell you."

The splash was followed by silence.

"Johnny?"

Silence and the gliding away of two ducks were all that could be heard.

"Johnny? Johnny? Johnny!!!"

The questioning voice turned into a panic stricken scream that echoed around the river, hitting the Abbey and sending a shivering howl into the night sky. The eyes of the mother searched desperately for a sign of her son, but none was to be seen in the black waters of the river.

At the far end on the river, the two ducks sailed effortlessly into a hidden cave, causing no ripples or noise as they pushed through the leaves of an overhanging Weeping Willow.

The only noise that could be heard in the still night air was that of a mother, quietly repeating the name of her son over and over in bewilderment.

"Johnny!"

The two ducks pushed into the depths of the cave, deep into its mouth where the water became shallower and the mud started to cling to their down.

As they got further in, the sides of the cave pushed in and on the natural shelves appeared the occasional mallard. As they went further in, the numbers of mallards grew and, within the last hundred yards, the walls were covered in quacking, chattering ducks, dark eyes piercing the gloom to see the two arrivals and to assess their evening's work.

The quacking built to a crescendo, echoing menacingly around the dark walls of the cave as they waddled to their feet in the shallow water.

The two reached the end of the cave. Above them, almost like a balcony in a theatre, sat up to one hundred ducks, quacking in excited anticipation. Suddenly they fell silent as a large, dark, shifting form began to rouse itself.

One hundred times the size of the other ducks, the dark shape slowly moved and a massive, black eye blinked to life. A beak the size of a car flashed in the gloom. Blood could be seen to drip from it as it jerked to a halt, eyeing the new arrivals.

The two ducks visibly quaked, hoping that the gift they had brought would meet with acceptance. They had seen the anger of the beast before and had lost friends and colleagues who had failed to please the large duck with their sacrifices.

They dumped their quarry and held their breath for the judgment. They eyed each other nervously.

The large shape moved and, with one eye, analysed the offering. Slowly, its beak opened. Wider and wider.

A rancid, echoing roar bounced around the cave, followed by excited quacking from the other ducks, making a deafening cacophony of bloodletting acceptance.

The two ducks breathed a sigh of relief and slipped back into the water, breathing calmly again, allowing the large shape time to enjoy its feast in peace.

The noise carried on long into the night, drowned out to the outside world by some rather clever soundproofing that many people would recognise as duck droppings.

ONE

What is a nightmare and when does it ever end? Is it a sleeping phenomenon or can it carry on into wakefulness? Am I actually asleep or am I awake? And how many beans make five?

My own personal nightmare came unexpectedly upon me. Life, as it had so far been, had been unremarkable and I was quite unready for what was to come over the months and maybe years following the first incident.

I lived alone. An unexceptional life, the tedium only occasionally interrupted by bouts of wind and the sporadic itchy rash behind my knee. Oh, and the unannounced visits from my Great Aunt Augusta, an eccentric woman in the old mould, who insisted on travelling everywhere by horse, despite the predominance of the motor car and the fact that she didn't own a horse herself. Property, she said, was theft, which went some way to explaining my regular visits to the police station to bail her and somebody else's horse out. It was a sad sight on a Saturday night to see an old woman and her horse behind bars. It was an even sadder one to see an old woman and somebody else's horse behind bars, both handcuffed together.

"Hiawatha, my golden steed!" my great Aunt Augusta would cry as we walked down the High Street, my pockets light through bail money again, "Where is my golden steed?"

I did not have the heart to tell her that she was sitting on the beast itself.

This Sunday, for it was a Sunday when it all began, my Great Aunt was not visiting me, so I really don't know why I mentioned her.

This Sunday, the day the nightmare began, was a cold, autumnal day, although it wasn't autumn. The grey waters of the river rumbled quietly in the dwindling sunlight, shafts of light catching and glaring from time to time as I walked along the river bank.

It was surprisingly quiet, peaceful and tranquil as Sundays should be.

But this Sunday was about to be different. Although it gave no hint of menace or horror, it was about to lurch into unforgiving terror, terror that would effect the lives of an entire nation. I blinked, innocently, into the pale sunny sky.

Eric, my constant companion in a world that no longer considered loyalty something worthwhile, was at my side. He bounded ahead of me, on all fours, which would have been a strange sight had he not have been a Labrador, which, thankfully, he was. An honest, innocent Labrador who barked and yelped joyously, contentedly, oblivious to the horror that awaited him.

As I have already stated, my life until this moment had been uneventful to the point of mind-numbing tedium. I lived in Knaresborough, a small town in Yorkshire with little to recommend it, which suited me fine. I was not a Yorkshire man, having travelled north when just a baby with my parents, a couple who were not loving but caring in a really boring sort of way. They moved back to the South shortly after and shortly returned again to Yorkshire to collect me from the Dry-Cleaners where they had absent-mindedly left me.

They led a nomadic life and from time to time I actually caught up with them. I had settled in Knaresborough some three years previously, having little contact with anybody, which suited me and, by their two-fingered salutes, them.

My only real companions were the aforementioned Great Aunt Augusta, who believed Eric to be a rather large goldfish whom she had met in a previous existence, and Eric, who knew he wasn't and who realised what a crushing bore I was. He preferred it that way and so did I.

Never having seen the high life, I never longed for it. Excitement was unknown to me. The steady and unchanging pace of life here suited me fine. Never had I longed for fame or fortune, never had I wished for a jet-setting executive's life with nights on the town and dalliances with those ladies who would gladly take their clothes off in return for a bottle of rather expensive champagne that would have brought about a bilious attack that would have forced me into the plush bathroom with the marbled sink and bath the size of the Atlantic. Never had I yearned for the type of attention you get from those Oriental ladies from Bangkok or wherever it was, you know, the type you read about in the Sunday papers but never quite manage to encounter yourself, unless you count the young daughter of the woman who runs the take-away, the one who struggles working out the change for Chicken Fried Rice on a Friday night, whom you shouldn't really think of in that way because she is quite respectable, I suppose.

I was quite content, thank you, with my tedious life and my friendship with my dog in my one bed roomed flat with the anaglypta wallpaper and a steady job.

This idyllic life was about to shatter.

Eric bounded out of view. His breath hung alone in the air. I called him. There was no reply.

Surveying the scene all I could see were the trees and the river, the former moving slowly in the breeze and the latter reflecting the sparkling sun.

I craned my head and scratched it in bewilderment, which is a good trick if you can get away with it. But I could not see my dog anywhere. I scratched my head again, keeping my gloves on so as to avoid injury. I shouted him; normally this causes him to return immediately, but not today. No noise, no sign, nothing. Mysterious.

Suddenly, the sky darkened menacingly. A cold chill blew around my legs, up my overcoat and into my boxer shorts, making me shiver.

My heart began to beat faster and louder. Red panic crept over me; I shouted for Eric again, but there was no response. My cries became increasingly anxious. The wind stiffened. All of nature seemed to suddenly gel into a fierce figure of burning hate, or at least something quite like that. I felt exposed to the elements, aware that Mother Nature herself was ill at ease with the change in the surroundings.

The trees bent, dolefully, under the weight of the suddenly icy breeze; the river rippled white under the small shafts of sunlight that poked through the billowing clouds. I quaked at the all-embracing and ultimately terrifying power that nature could unleash.

I was helpless to stop it. I felt strangely vulnerable.

The air fell silent. The wind dropped as a solitary bird screeched across the sky, fleeing the scene. The moored boats, vehicles of entertainment throughout the summer, bobbled and bashed into the bank below, onomatopoetically.

The rustling reeds that ran along the bank bowed in the whistling wind, onomatopoeically, exposing the four ducks and the frantic paddling of a Labrador.

"The frantic paddling of a Labrador?" I repeated to myself. "Eric? Eric? Eric!!!!"

But it was too late. Below me, in the river, Eric swam a desperate stroke, crashing and splashing, trying in vain to ward off the jabbing attentions of four ducks which tore at his golden coat with their evil, jig-sawing bills. Blood fountained into the air, bubbling into the river, covering Eric and his assailants. Red water splashed and circled around.

I saw all of this in slow motion, though it could only have taken seconds. The ducks efficiently pulled at his flesh, ripping him apart carefully in a frenzied yet calculated manner before leaving his bobbing carcass to float lifelessly down the river into the reddening tide.

Quacking triumphantly, they splashed a joyous dance of death in the blood red waters below me.

The sun was cut out as, above me, a massive black cloud of ducks hovered overhead. The four ducks, hearing the evil cackle of their blood thirsty relations above, looked skywards. It was then, and only then, I caught the menace in their black, empty eyes. Eyes that knew no compassion, eyes that could see no love, eyes that lusted after blood.

The four flapped into the sky, their bills dripping with the blood of my only companion, to join their massed bands of destruction which moved on, ready and waiting for the on-coming blitz that the world knew nothing of.

A low cackle of impending doom could be heard. I gulped a slow gulp. I knew my nightmare had begun. As yet, few others knew that my nightmare would soon become theirs but soon this cloud of death would descend to bring death and destruction on a scale not normally associated with ducks.

The River Craven ran politely through Skipton, swelled by the early April showers. A rainbow circled the town, unseen by the early morning shoppers, unused to sun or warmth at this time of year. The town buzzed slowly awake, shops clattering their doors open, shopkeepers complaining into the mist of the morning. The first cars spluttered to life and the trucks airbroke to a halt or bundled themselves over the humped bridges throughout the town.

The smell of fresh daffodils wafted down to the canal side as Stenton Broomstalker opened the brightly-painted door of his barge, "The Donger", his retirement present to himself. He had retired early, surprised that his company could dispense with his invaluable services so early and so keenly. Now free from the shackles of working life, Stenton was determined to make his lasting impression on the world. He had set himself up as a travelling artist, sketching and oiling local scenes with all of the skill of a blind mud-wrestler on an acid trip.

Stenton was not content with inflicting his "talent" on the world; he had also set up a "Painting Co-operative" to provide "meaningful support" for "struggling talent". So far the take-up for his offer had been scant to the point of nil.

Stenton opened the doors of his barge and breathed in the fresh diesel filled air. Coughing loudly, he tripped up the stairs leading from his bedroom and blinked into the sun, his thoughts drifting to the prospect of a day's cruising up to the hills of Craven and the towering rocks of Malham.

Turning towards the galley and his breakfast, he glanced and smiled at the ducks gathering around the neighbouring barge, "Dundrivin". As a car bumped over the bridge above, Stenton sighed at the strange calm of the canal so close to the bustling centre of modern commerce above. It was one of Yorkshire's strange contradictions that there could be ducks, the playful side of the conundrum called life, so close to the man-made mess above. How could the human world so carelessly mess itself up whilst the ducks kept their innocence? Stenton thought of painting the scene but quickly recalled the problems he had painting animals. And scenery. And buildings. And human beings. Most things, to be honest, unless it was vaguely abstract and even that could be a struggle.

Within minutes, the bacon crackled and spat in the frying pan. Stenton sat on deck, lapping up the sun's early rays. Over in "Dundrivin" Angus McManus, retired coalman and poems, whistled contentedly in his strange Scottish brogue as he dangled his feet in the river, painting the hull of his barge between his legs. Angus, white-whiskered and red-nosed, was a local character and now aged eighty-three. He liked to recite his poems to anyone who had the time to listen but these bordered on the pornographic, embellished by adverbs and adjectives that used more "f"s than you could shake a stick at, if that's your idea of a good time.

"Lovely morning, isn't it?" Stenton shouted breezily.

Angus, keeping eye contact to a minimum, spat a large clump of phlegm playfully into the river.

"Makes you want to compose, doesn't it?"

"Ye should decompose," spat Angus to himself under his breath, "that would be good!"

"A wonderful day, a day in which poems should be written and stanzas, erm, stanzaered."

"Bog off," replied Angus and muttered something rude.

Stenton smiled at this witty response. "Like the first day of spring, isn't it?"

"It is the first day of spring you half baked excuse for a human being," replied Angus.

Stenton smiled back awkwardly.

"Well, can't stand round here all day talking, I've got bacon to eat and, erm, things," shouted Stenton, retreating to the galley once more.

"Go fry yer spotty bum," growled Angus.

Down in the galley, Stenton smiled as he thought of the great aura of companionship he felt with Angus; he was not fooled by his frosty exterior that belied a lifetime of friendship that he had managed to build over almost two days moored by Angus. He was friendly in an off-hand way admittedly, but he didn't fool Stenton. It was difficult to fool Stenton; he did too good a job of it himself.

"I wonder if he'd like some bacon," he thought as he laid three rashers of bacon on a day old wholemeal cob and covered then with tomato sauce. "I'll take him some out to him."

Once he got up on deck, he looked around but Angus was nowhere to be seen. All Stenton could see was Angus' brush floating face down in the river surrounded by a small wreath of red paint.

"Angus! Angus!" shouted Stenton but there was no reply. This was strange. Stenton was used to the "Bog off" response that Angus normally so playfully used in a matey type of way, but he hadn't heard this, even though it was placidly quiet.

Too quiet. No movement. Nothing.

Stenton wondered what to do. So he decided to eat the bacon himself.

As he lowered himself into the galley again, four ducks circled the barge. As Stenton reached the top of the stairs, he was engulfed in a flurry of feathers and blood as the ducks clinically took his life and his bacon sandwich from him.

Stenton never knew what hit him.

Which just proved Angus right.

Even in death, Stenton was an ignorant fart.

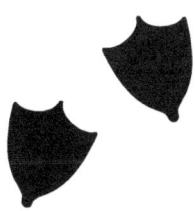

In the old landmark, the two black birds looked at each other. They knew something was up but, as usual, their feeders didn't. Okay, so their feeders *thought* that they had clipped their wings and that they couldn't fly away but they knew differently. Their feeders weren't bright; they did look after captive birds, after all, how bright do you have to be?

The two black birds looked at each other. Of course, they couldn't talk but they could communicate.

One looked at its wing as if at a watch and moved its head.

The other winked, knowingly.

They stayed were they where for the time being as the tourists were flocking in, but they knew that they wouldn't be around for long at this rate, unless those idiots on two legs realized what was going on, which they probably wouldn't. So, you see, if you are stupid, chances are history will teach you nothing.

TWO

It felt as if time was standing still as I raced towards the police station, my head spinning from the scene I had just left behind on the banks of the normally placid River Nidd. As in a dream, my legs moved slowly but took me nowhere at all, legs made seemingly of lead and no matter how quickly I ran, I could not get where I wanted to be.

It was an awful feeling, a gut wrenching experience. My brain swam in a sea of emotions as I desperately tried to reach my intended goal but I moved, slowly, slowly, oh so slowly as if I could not control my destiny at all. I couldn't. My foot was stuck in a grid.

I freed my foot and tumbled towards the police station, a beacon of salvation in my nightmare of death. Well, it would have been, but, in fact, it was closed.

"You alright, guv?" asked a policeman, getting into a car.

"No, well, I, you see, if, that is..." I began, shaking.

"That's alright then," he continued, getting into the car and starting it up.

"No!" I screamed, leaping onto the car and banging at the windscreen.

The policeman wound down the window.

"Is everything alright, sir?" he asked me.

"Well, no, you see, down at the river, my dog and, well, the ducks and, blood, foam, gnashing of bills, erm..."

The policeman looked at me. "Could this wait until the morning, sir, but I've just locked up, you see and it's a bit of a fuss to have to reset the alarm and things."

I stared at him. Long and hard. Through the windscreen. Even when the windscreen wipers went on. And the screen-wash splashed over me.

"Perhaps you might like to get into the car, sir."

I removed myself from the bonnet of the car and got into it.

"Perhaps the passenger side would be the better option, sir."

I moved to the other side of the car and started to tell my story. He looked at me incredulously but took notes of my experiences as I rambled on. It took me five minutes to relate the terrible tale of the minutes before.

"So, sir," he said in summary, "a group of ducks savaged your dog to death, you say?"

"No," I replied.

"No, sir?"

"No, I said a flock of ducks, not a group. The collective noun for ducks is flock, not group."

"Are you sure?" asked the policeman. "I thought it was group or at least gaggle."

"Gaggle of geese."

"Well, make your mind up. Was it ducks or geese?"

"It was ducks!"

"So it wasn't geese?"

"I never said it was geese, I said it was a hoard of ducks."

"It's never a hoard, sir. I don't think that's a collective noun for anything and certainly not for ducks. A hoard of collectors or a hoard of kleptomaniacs, maybe, but not ducks, certainly not ducks. I'll tell you what, I'll just put a lot of ducks, if that's okay with you."

"Well," I exasperated, "that's fine, just go and arrest them!"

There was a rather long and silent silence. The policeman looked at me. Quizzically. For a long time. And then he spoke.

"Arrest them, sir?"

"Erm...yes. Well, perhaps not arrest them, exactly, but, erm, do something, I suppose," I responded, somewhat weakly.

"Like?" the policeman asked with just a hint of sarcasm in his voice. "Any ideas?"

I looked blank at him and smiled a pathetic smile.

"Tell them off, perhaps?" he asked me.

"But you don't realise. This is an isolated incident that could well have terrible portents for the future. Although this is only the death of a dog I would not be at all surprised to find that this is a precursor to a larger threat to all of mankind since the viciousness portrayed by these ducks, these devil ducks, showed a frightening lack of care for life that I found unusual for beasts that are normally perceived as rather peaceful and quacking things."

The policeman looked at me even longer and harder.

"And if they can kill a dog then they can kill a human being. It's just the next small step. Good god, they may even have started already. Have you got any unsolved murders or disappearances perhaps?"

This was met with an even more incredulous look.

"Well?!"

I realised I was screaming a little. Well, a lot, really. So I shouldn't have been too surprised to find myself thrown into a cell, despite the hassle with the alarm. The only thing I was surprised at was being charged with solvent abuse and desperate plot exposition.

"Ducks, I ask you. As if ducks could kill anyone, they are such cuddly, placid things," he mumbled as he locked the door. "What type of glue is it you are using, sir... powerful, is it?"

"No, please believe me... go on, check your files. I bet you've got some unsolved deaths lately. Really strange ones. Ones you can't understand."

"Of course we've got some of them," he replied, "it is a police station, after all."

The keys jangled heavily in the lock as it locked.

I was left alone all night.

I awoke screaming. Unaware of my strange surroundings I leapt to the floor and yelled for my freedom, screaming, shouting, pleading for someone to release me, someone to understand my plight.

"Let me out, for pity's sake, let me out!" I bellowed.

A young constable stood at the cell door, unmoved.

"Let me out," I sobbed, somewhat pitifully.

There was a pause as our eyes met.

"Actually, you'll find that the door's open, always is, can be dangerous locking people up. They can turn quite violent, don't you know?" he said quite matter of factly.

I slowly rose to my feet, trying to compose an air of dignity through my blushes.

"Good, fine, many thanks. Amateur dramatics, you see. Shakespeare next week. King Lear. Getting some practice in. Blow winds and all of that. Erm, can I go, then?"

"Go where?"

"Free, perhaps?"

"If you want. Got a busy day here today. Apparently there was some sort of murder here last night."

I quaked and looked at him in terror.

"Murder?" I asked.

"Yes. Or was it burglary? Which is the one where things get stolen, I always tend to get mixed up?"

"Erm... burglary."

"Oh, it was that then. Not murder after all. Still, quite a lot taken from a pet shop. Mysterious, really, no money, just lots of bird food."

"Bird food?" I asked.

"Yes."

"Any leads?"

"No, just bird food. Must rush. Got to go and help, see yourself out."

I tried to but didn't get far. Just as I was about to exit the police station, two plain clothed individuals appeared as if from nowhere and blocked my path. They towered above me and looked quietly in control with just a dash of threatening.

"Going somewhere are we?" the first asked.

"Erm, I thought so," I nervously replied.

"You're the one who's seen the ducks, are you?" asked the other, obviously playing inquisitive cop to the other's inquisitive cop.

The question startled me. I had forgotten about the ducks and the attack I had come to report. I mumbled a yes.

"Right, then, Charlie, you're coming with us."

I found myself lifted off my feet and bundled into a brightly lit, clinical room. At the solitary table sat a solitary man, holding a teddy bear. He looked up, bulbous eyes piercing my own terrified gaze.

"By the way, my name's not Charlie," I pointed out to a blank response.

He nodded to the two men who had bundled me in. They nodded back. He nodded again. They nodded back again. He nodded more furiously. They returned the nod. He nodded three times, almost violently and they returned the nod.

There was short silence.

"Get out!!! That nod means get out!!" the solitary man screamed. "My head hurts now..."

"Oh," the two replied in unison. "Are you sure? I thought get out was two nods?"

He nodded a reply. Then tutted. They made for the door and halted. They turned and looked at the solitary man.

"Positive?" one asked.

"Could be dangerous," added the other.

The solitary man nodded again and banged his head on the desk. The two men left, quickly.

The solitary man took a pencil from the pocket in his white coat and sucked it slowly. His eyes very gradually met with mine and he motioned for me to sit down, which I did. This solitary man was some sort of psychologist. He'd long forgotten what type, though "clinical" sounded good, so he used that. He wanted to join the police force many years before but was rejected for being too noisy, which seemed a strange reason to reject him. But he learned from this and toned down his ties accordingly. He was, ironically for a psychologist, a mental wreck. He'd had a bad home life, he had three broken relationships (one with a woman, one with a man and one with a rocking horse) and it had left him deeply scarred. And scared, for that matter. He grew a beard to hide his fear and kept it tidy but it didn't really help. He knew that, of course, but he was trying to fool himself. Or, at least, he thought he was trying to fool himself. That's the problem about being a psychologist, the double bluff seldom works. "Or does it?" he asked himself, maybe rhetorically. Triple bluffs seldom work, either.

There was a long silence. It was time for an opening gambit.

"So, you've seen a UFO, have you?" he asked.

"No," I replied.

"Neither have I," he returned, slowly and confidently. "So, what IS IT you have seen?"

His emphasis was wildly incorrect.

"Do you know what I do?" he asked me, quietly without eye contact. I answered in the negative, since I didn't. "Very clever reply. I am a clinical psychologist. I can tell you why you are mad. I can tell you why I am mad. I can explain the entire world in three minutes and make sense of all the nonsense in the world. Are you impressed?"

"Erm, I suppose so."

"Yes, I can do all this. But, you know, I always have to buy slip on shoes as I have terrible trouble understanding shoe laces. Don't you find that they're... tricky?"

I had to admit that I did not find them so.

"Ah-ha! So, how long have you suffered from this feeling of superiority to figures of authority?"

He looked at me straight with cold but caring eyes and a crooked smile that was insincerity incarnate.

"I know what I'm talking about you know. I've got a white coat. And a teddy bear. His name is Malcolm. So is mine."

"I thought you were going to ask me about the ducks," I blurted out, just getting a little worried now.

At the sound of the word ducks he became agitated and annoyed. He leaped from his chair and walked around muttering "ducks, mallards, ducks" very loudly under his breath, if this isn't an oxymoron. Just as suddenly as he rose he sat down again and collected his thoughts. He looked at me again. He stroked his tidy beard. And he shouted.

"Ducks, you say. *ARE YOU* mocking *ME*? Ducks. *DUCKS*! I *HAVE* seen ducks myself! In ones, in twos, in sevens, some holding hands, some petting, some playing billiards. Why, only last weekend in Otley marketplace I saw thousands *OF THEM*, milling around, *MILLING*, quacking, quacking their death quack in terrifying unison. We are *DOOMED*, doomed, *DOOMED*. I tell you we *ARE* doomed."

He sat, eyes agape, mouth ajar, at the edge of his seat.

"We are doomed and no one will listen. We shall all be *KILLED* by ducks!!!"

There was a pause of indeterminable length.

"Not really plausible, though. Not Freudian enough for me. Now, if it would have been snakes we had been talking about, well, that would be different..." he continued, quietly.

The door burst open and the two men from before entered.

"Sorry, wrong guy," they said and pulled me from the room. They dumped me outside of the police station and then picked me up and dumped me back into a cell.

The psychologist mouthed "Damn!" to himself and bit the end off his pencil, "just when we were getting somewhere."

I didn't know what to do. I was relieved that I was safe from the terror I had seen before but also terrified that I could not communicate what I knew to the outside world whilst stuck in a prison cell. And there was a nice cup of tea in the cell, too, which was useful.

A message crackled over the telephone.

"Hundreds, hundreds I tell you...it's carnage."

"Sorry, was that carpets you said?" asked the attractive but cerebrally challenged redhead at the end of the phone.

"No, carnage, carnage, C A R N A G E... carnage!"

"It's a very bad line. Is it a mobile you're on?"

"Of course it is! I'm standing in the middle of hundreds of dead bodies... apparently killed by ducks."

"Is that dogs you said?"

"No, ducks...D U C K S...ducks."

"Could you spell that?"

The station controller of the small but very useless Riding Television snatched the phone from the P.A. and barked down the phone for clarification. He stared in amazement.

"It's a bad line... ducks, you say. Any pictures?"

"No. Bloody ducks ate the camera man and took the camera."

"What! You let the camera go! They're expensive bits of kit, you know. Tell you what, try getting a VAT receipt on your way back and I won't deduct it from your salary."

He put the phone down.

"Ducks. Did he say ducks?"

"I thought he was reporting about carpets. Definitely carpets. And dogs or something. At least that's what I heard him say. Wasn't a good line though. Those phones are no good you know. Should get a real one and work from an office."

"Ducks. I'm sure he said ducks. We could have a scoop, Francine."

"Oh, good. Shall I get the petty cash out again?""

THREE

Few people who passed the Nuclear Tracking Centre on their journey through the picturesque North Yorkshire Moors on the road to their holiday haunts in Bridlington, Filey and beyond ever realised the importance of the rather ramshackle building and the even more rather weather beaten green gate, despite the large metal reflectors which protruded out from the untended privet hedges that made up the perimeter fence of the Government owned establishment. There were two reasons for this. Firstly, it had been cunningly designed to be absolutely obvious in a game of reverse psychology that even the Russians, at the height of the cold war, thought must be a triple bluff, if not a quintuple one, if that was at all possible. Secondly, the sign that said "Nuclear Tracking Station" had fallen into the ditch at the side of the road.

Standing in isolated isolation in the red-poppied fields of wind-blown rape, there was a small Accommodation Area (living quarters), skulking in the shadow of a massive Electricity Supply Line (massive pylon) which helped to carry power to the station and its Nuclear Tracking Devices (large metal things that moved if the electricity was turned on). There were four such devices (reflectors), each pointing in a separate direction, turning slowly to track the world's skies, except for one, which pointed towards the rather mucky pond, as it had done since those nasty winds of the year before last. And the one which was permanently pointing up, never to move, since the heat-wave the year before, when somebody realised that it would make a good swimming pool.

That was the way Mr. Davies liked to run the Government establishment.

The Mr. Davies in question was a corpulent, sloppy man who looked like he had been born in his fifties and probably had been. He was short and unkempt and he wore loud ties, even with ill-fitting polo shirts. He had a moustache and a son, but not always in that order. He no longer had a wife. She had decided to leave them both almost three years before, bored at the total non-entity of the man she had married twelve years before. Coupled to which, she was a trainee nymphomaniac with a firm of local accountants.

Mr. Davies, or Frank as he was known to his seven year old son despite the fact that his name was Jeffrey, had never really missed his wife. Indeed, he hadn't realised she had left him until the doll she had put in their bed as she left (not as a gift, but a statement) had a puncture and flew wildly across the bedroom one night as he attempted his rather pathetic attempts at marital pleasures, a much mis-named concept in this case. And he wouldn't even have known then had his son not pointed out that his mum wasn't in fact either deflated or dead but living in Norton with a man called Beard, or something.

Frank, or Jeffrey, had only really missed his wife when it came to the washing up, as the kitchen bore testimony to. Here there were three years worth of unwashed plates and cutlery, coupled with an aroma of the armpit of a skunk's rather unpleasant elder dead brother. He had toyed with the idea of disposable plates but, rather logically, reasoned that if he couldn't wash real plates he'd never get around to washing unreal ones. It was the sort of logic his son had got used to.

As you may have gathered, Mr. Davies was an annoying, smelly, pointless individual, being slightly less than one-dimensional in character with all the conversational qualities of a broken vacuum cleaner which is lacking a plug and those nice attachments for doing settees and curtains.

How he ever became Operational Director of the Nuclear Tracking Centre was a mystery to most, probably even himself, especially as he had not had a distinguished career since leaving University with a degree in Inner City Stress Counseling (Honours Deferred). His last job, Assistant Marketing Assistant at Hasta Manana Spanish Spoon and Other Cutlery Company, had ended fairly quickly, the official reason, quoted in the letter from Head of Personnel, being that he "was a remarkably boring person with the ability to atrophy a banana from forty paces", which was not a talent open to question. Maybe this actually gave him the perfect attributes for this role as it entailed never coming into contact with any human beings, or so his bosses said. Maybe they were just protecting themselves from terminal boredom. But that did not help his son, the only person he ever saw.

Isambard, as his son was embarrassingly called, knew that his father was overbearingly boring, so tried to avoid him at all times. At seven, he was amazingly self-sufficient, which was through necessity rather than choice. With a father who had his head buried into a wall of visual display units, some of which actually worked, all day long, it was down to Isambard to keep himself alive and interested in life. He did.

Occasionally he had communication with his father. Well, to be honest, now and again his father would bellow "We are not being attacked again" or "There's hardly a trace of nuclear fall-out currently, you know" to no-one in particular.

Isambard preferred to spend his days sitting outside, throwing over-ripened oranges at the sheep grazing around the large metal things. This was unrewarding at the best of times; even if he hit a sheep, and he didn't do that too often, they just carried on chewing and being sick into the large metal things, but it was better than trying to forge filial bonds with an over-weight and over-poweringly boring father.

Isambard reasoned that life was bigger than himself, that this learning experience of his formative years, though emotionally scarring, would prove to have some positive element later in life, rounding his character for fruition at some stage in his late twenties, so must be perceived in a positive light.

He was quite a little sod, Isambard.

Today he was sitting in the window seat, counting sheep and oranges in the next field as the drivers on the road ploughed through the drizzle on their way to the coast and beyond when there was a knock on the door. Isambard opened the door and there was a duck.

"Wait there," said Isambard, "I'll get my dad. Dad, there's a duck at the door!"

There was a very short pause.

"Don't be incorrect, oh son of mine," came the response from Mr. Davies in his usual high-pitched drawl, "it must be a man with a bill!"

Isambard smacked his forehead. The duck dived into the green lights of the visual display units. Mr. Davies' life was tugged from him amidst a blaze of fluorescent flashing and fat screams, or was that flat screens?

The duck, its job completed, walked slowly up the hall, its bill dripping with blood, its wings shaking with murderous passion and leaped into the air to fly away.

As it did so, Isambard threw a piece of orange at it. He missed.

Just after nine o'clock the following morning, Knaresborough Town Hall clock struck nine.

"Late as usual," mused the burly policeman who was escorting me to the scene of that terrible incident of the day before.

I had spent the night half asleep, with nightmares disturbing me at regular intervals, sharing a cell with an Irish Forgery Expert, brought to book for unconvincing Ten Pound notes which not only had dates on but also spelled £ as "lb".

"No-one's perfect," he so correctly stated, pointing out that his brother had been imprisoned for a similar offence, filing down fifty pence pieces to make twenty pence pieces. He told me this as he dug a tunnel with a spoon from his breakfast tray.

I made conversation with him. It was better than the harrowing nightmares, but only just.

"Are you trying to escape?" I asked, somewhat rhetorically.

"Yes," he replied.

"Got very far?"

Oh, yes. Last time I got under the river."

"Really?" I blinked in amazement. "With a spoon?"

"Don't be daft! You couldn't get that far with just a spoon you big fat idjit! I had a knife and fork as well."

"And the police didn't suspect anything?"

"Oh, no. Kept them at bay. Couldn't find the tunnel as I filled it in each night. Fooled 'em completely."

I had been taken away from the forger at first light, to come to the scene of the incident the day before and fully explain what had happened. As we reached the river the policeman who accompanied me stopped to survey the bleak, grey scene.

"We're not too impressed with your story, you know," he told me. "No sign of a body. Can't do much without a body."

I didn't listen, I could only look at the gurgling waters, swelled by the heavy rain of the night before, and recall the horror of the day before.

"So, you see, there is no evidence, no evidence at all."

"But it happened, it happened here, it happened yesterday, it did!" I implored.

He looked unimpressed. As he looked up and down the banks of the river he could see not one duck, either mallard or teal and I had to agree that there was a surfeit of lack of evidence. But how could I get him to understand what had happened yesterday? How could I get anyone to understand? Indeed, had it really happened? Had I just dreamed it? Yes, I had seen it, it wasn't a dream. I winced as I thought of the ducks tearing into my dear, dead, departed dog with awesome, terrifying power and ferocity.

"Not one shred of evidence," he said again as he toppled, slowly, head over heel into the grey, gurgling river below.

"No!" I thought to myself, "the ducks again!"

"Help! Help!!" he screamed as he splashed about but before my trembling hands could come to his assistance three ducks appeared, as from nowhere, to savage the drowning policeman and haul his struggling body up the river to a screaming, horrible, lingering, wet and bloody death.

I stood, amazed, dazed and terrified again, as I had been yesterday. Once again it seemed that I was in the presence of the beasts of the devil.

"Ah, bloody hell and all, not again," came a voice from below my feet.

Looking down, I recognised the face of last night's cellmate, protruding from the man-hole cover on which the unfortunate policeman had been standing just seconds before. He blinked into the sunlight, face darkened with mud.

"Wrong darned side again. That's twice now! But I was close. Could have been worse, could have been in the river. Oh, hello there."

I stood amazed. He didn't know what had happened, hadn't seen the ducks and could not have been a witness. Yet again, I was the only one who knew. And I feared the worst: these devil ducks *were* a major threat to the well being of the country if not the entire world. The ducks were, as they say, here.

So was the tunnel digging Irishman.

"Ah, look will you, I've gone and bent my spoon. Damn. Haven't got one on you, have you?"

I looked down at him, mouth agape. He must have thought I was deranged, which, indeed, I felt I was especially as, above his head, I could make out the shape of a solitary duck.

He didn't suspect anything. The beak hit his head and cracked it wide open, spilling blood all over the bank. He smiled strangely before he, too, toppled into the river, closely followed by the duck and his blood thirsty chums.

I ran. Like hell. The nightmare really had begun.

In the large park the couple walked hand-in-hand in the dying light of the early spring evening, passing the lake, unaware of the lingering danger that lurked in the banks below their feet.

In between the rowing boats bobbled a mallard, blood dripping from its beak. It held its breath as it heard the approach of human blood and smiled a duck-like smile.

It quivered slightly in anticipation of its prey. The light caught its dark, brooding eye. It held its breath and bided its time. Seeing an opportunity, it glided up to the reeds and lay patiently in wait.

The couple came nearer and nearer.

The young man stopped. The duck saw its chance. It braced itself, slowly and quietly opening its wings and pushing itself into the darkening air.

At that moment, the young man decided that the time was right and, unaware of the impending danger, fell down onto one knee, ready to plight his troth to his female beloved. As he did so, the duck zoomed above his head and clattered both noisily and fatally into a tree.

The young man looked up and stared.

"What's up?" asked his beloved.

"Oh, erm, my shoe lace needed doing up," he said, getting up and scratching his head. "Was that a duck?"

His beloved looked at him.

"I think you need to keep off the lager," she said in response.

"Hey, drivers, how's the traffic?" gushed the drive time DJ. "Let me and mad Sally know, yes, that's mad Sally and me, Mad Charlie Charles, so good they named me twice!"

Mad Charlie Charles was actually Christopher Silly but he changed his name by deed poll when he got a job at the local radio station. Which was weird, as his employers had actually employed him mostly because of his surname. Okay, so he did have a track record on local hospital radio but that was mostly for the higher number of reported deaths on the ward during his show, mostly through overdoses and hardly any through heart attacks brought on by endless mirth. But you can make statistics say anything and Christopher did. Though not in an amusing way.

He had now "done" the drive time show for three weeks and had already managed to annoy all of the staff at the radio station, all four, that is. Sally hated him and had recently put washing up liquid in his coffee, telling him they had a new cappuccino machine.

"Really," he replied, "I didn't even know you liked monkeys!"

He was off the next day with a bad bout of "jippy tummy" and the listening figures went up.

His producer, Bert Scaup, hated him too and gave him the worst music play-list ever thought up to play. The highlight was The Singing Nun with "Dominique" though there were many other lowlights, put into the shade only by Charlie's irritating content and monotone delivery style.

"He thinks he's mad, he's just crap," Bert was once heard to say, on air, direct to Charlie.

Charlie thought the world was mad. Mad meaning "crazy".

"I'm not mad," mouthed Sally to the strawberry blonde DJ with a look of total distain.

"Well, drivers, it is five past five and here is Sally with all of the news on the roads! How are the roads tonight, Sally?"

Sally thought of a very good use for a gun at that time. Or at least a banana and some Vaseline. Or putty.

"Well," started Sally.

"They're well? You sure?" interrupted Mad Charlie Charles.

She mouthed "shut up" and made a rude gesture with her hand as she carried on. "Ha-ha, no, Charlie, it's *NOT* good news, in fact, it's mostly carnage out there due to ducks."

"Sorry, Sally, I thought you did say ducks?"

"Yes, I did, cloth ears..."

"Ha-ha!!"

"...ducks. Ducks are causing hold ups throughout the country though only in small pockets of the country at the moment, not yet widespread and, let's face it, not here in the great metropolis..."

"The great metrolops, as I call it!"

".. so who cares. Unless you're headed north, of course."

"Who'd do that? Know what I mean. North? You are kidding!! So, Sally, ready for a drink after the show? Charlie is, as he always is, ready!"

"No."

"Ha-ha, so you'll be back in an hour, Sally?"

"Hopefully not."

"Ha-ha!! That's Sally, always messing us about. What a card! She loves me really, we have a great working relationship, listeners, we really do."

Sally smiled and wafted a single finger in the air, aimed at Charlie Charles, as she left.

Mad Charlie Charles let out a fake laugh and played his Mad Charlie Charles jingle.

"And that's our Sally, always flirting. And the next record is one I like to flirt to..." prattled on Mad Charlie Charles not realizing that, as Sally had left, so a small duck had waddles into the studio.

As Bert his producer chatted with Sally in the booth beyond, Charlie Charles carried on his meaningless chatter to anyone who couldn't change their car radio, oblivious to the duck climbing onto the studio controls and closer to his neck.

"Well, what do we have next," asked Charlie as the track faded out, "why it's..."

And suddenly, the radio signal beamed silence across the nation, his producer flirted with Sally and Mad Charlie Charles had broadcast his last programme.

All was silent and hardly anyone cared.

Looking up, the producer, realizing there was dead air, hit a button and Disco Duck by Ricky Lee and his Cast of Idiots suddenly filled the musical void.

Ironically.

I got home and locked the door behind me.

I daren't put on the television or the radio, as neither would fit me.

I didn't know what the future held for me and the world, I didn't even know if there was a future.

I just knew that I was afraid. Very afraid.

Luckily, I always had spare toilet roll, which I knew would come in useful in the coming days.

FOUR

The surgery of Dr. Garganey, as they often phrased it in third rate chillers like what this book is turning into, sat on the edge of the seedier side of the smoky and sprawling Northern conurbation. Although it was hardly a glamorous position (his mother thought it was "below him", quite an easy feat as he himself was almost seven feet tall), it was good for business, if pretty awful for staff morale. His staff gave a new definition to the phrase "all time low" and it looked as though some had dug a ditch to help this low get lower. Naturally, the large Dr. Garganey wasn't too worried about that as he was, in his eye at least, a manager of people, which meant that the feelings of the people were not paramount, especially if they were staff or patients or anybody who wasn't him. After all, he either paid them or cured them, at least in his eye, which was only partially correct, even on a good day.

The surgery had seen better days but it avoided the cliché of normal surgeries by having up-to-date newspapers in the waiting room. Up to date free newspapers, admittedly, but they were up to date. This didn't help distract from the peeling paint on the crumbling yellow walls and the curling Formica on the receptionist's desk which seemed to jump at every cough and sneeze from the ever-waiting patients. Mrs. Elsna Green, the similarly crumbling and curling receptionist who may well have been made out of Formica herself, coughed and sneezed in harmony with the patients, as, over the years, she had developed a strange immunity to the endless drugs the good doctor had decided best for her.

The same could be said of the doctor. He sat behind his curling and crumbling desk coughing and wheezing, using a large blue handkerchief to muzzle his snuffle, from time to time, as well as using the same cloth to clean his stethoscope. He pushed his red button to summon his next patient and Mrs. Green, a fifty seven year old "bachelor person", as she preferred to be known, flew into action (well, she looked at the next victim and nodded towards the yellowing Formica door, behind which sat the good doctor).

Dr. Garganey could not recall seeing his next patient recently; he was a man of indifferent age and ungainly walk who found it difficult to sit in the doctor's plastic chair without sliding off.

"Erm, good morning," he therefore said to Mr. Bewick, preferring this to the "Nice to see you again", which could lead to unforeseen complications, or the more common, "How are you then?", which normally lead to a bout of sarcasm that the good doctor could do without at nine twenty on a Tuesday morning. Either that or a reply that explained all the patient's ailments in such detail that the doctor often felt like replying "Hey, you'll find that I'm the doctor around here!".

"Is it?" replied Mr. Bewick.

"Erm, is what what?" retorted the doctor, who had judged his greeting as purely rhetorical and had therefore forgotten what he had originally said.

"I said, is it? A good morning, that is? I mean, it may be for you, but it is raining again and therefore does not fit into my category of good."

Dr.Garganey was somewhat taken aback by this response. Firstly, it was too early in the day. Secondly, most of his patients were incurably thick and probably thought a category was a place you put your pet when you went on holiday.

"Not unusual, since it's spring, but it is still an inaccurate description of the day as I see it from my current perspective."

Dr.Garganey thought of asking the man whether he was suffering from a nasty bout of verbal diarrhoea but resisted and instead asked the man his name.

"Bewick. Frank Bewick."

"So, erm how are you, Mr. Bewick?" asked the doctor, absent mindedly, forgetting his own rule of thumb never to ask this question of patients. There was a short pause and the doctor tried to kick himself between snuffles and wipes.

Bewick leaned across the desk.

"I feel like a duck," he said without a hint of anything in his voice.

The doctor, not too surprisingly, eyed him for a while, pondering a suitable reply, if, indeed there was one to such a comment.

"This, Mr. Bewick, is, unless I am mistaken, still a surgery, not a Chinese restaurant."

Bewick shoved his hands deep into the pockets of his large raincoat and ignored the reply. Bending his elbows, he began to flap like a duck, accompanying this with a loud and extremely accurate quacking sound.

"The other night," he began in conspiratorial tones, "I woke up, trembling and sweating. I had had the most horrible dream, nay, nightmare. I was sitting on the Town Hall steps in the middle of the night and I was..." and here he halted for dramatic effect "... I was totally surrounded by... ducks. Millions of them. Ducks, ducks and more ducks. But, doctor, not any old ducks. No. These were different. These were chomping and gnawing and quacking their bloody bills following a murderous feast. They were devil ducks, doctor, devil ducks, I tell you. Ducks from hell. It was... terrifying, terrifying. I woke up and there at the end of my bed was..."

The doctor, who had started out as a disinterested observer but had been now dragged into the drama of the narrative, finished the sentence for Mr. Bewick.

"A duck?!?" he blurted, trembling somewhat.

"Oh, no. It was Reginald, my Burmese cat. Why would it have been a duck? No, it was Reginald who was biting my big toe in an attempt to wake me as my screaming had woken him up and he'd had a particularly tough night on the tiles and needed his shut eye."

"Isn't that somewhat strange?" asked Dr. Garganey.

"Yes, it was! I never knew Reginald could speak!"

The doctor tutted, impatiently.

"I think you could do with a holiday," he said.

"On a lake, do you think?"

The doctor eyed him suspiciously. "Mr. Bewick," he replied, "do you ever get the urge to sit on eggs and... fly?"

"Of course!" Mr. Bewick replied, "do you?"

"And swim about on lakes?"

"Naturally."

"And, erm, from time to time eat soggy pieces of bread?"

"Yummy, yes!"

The doctor took off his glasses.

"And how long have you been like this, exactly?"

"Oh, ever since I was a duckling, I suppose."

The doctor threw his glasses down onto his desk and they scuttled off the pile of files and onto the floor, which was not quite what the good doctor intended. He looked at the author through the reams of paper and constant clatter of the word processor. He mumbled, quite audibly, about pathetically long build ups to obvious jokes as he stood up and took the shortest route out of the book he hadn't even asked to be in anyway, saying something about being in a James Herriot novel if he'd have been able to take up that job in North Yorkshire and how other authors would have made the best of his character, given more time and plot development.

The door slammed behind him. Plaster fell off the wall.

Mr.Bewick sat, alone, and somewhat awkwardly, in the doctor's room, waiting to see how the author would get him out of this mess.

Then he jumped up on the desk, quacked menacingly and leaped out of the open window to a certain death, had he not been on the first floor. He sprained his ankle/webbed foot.

I did not dare venture out for three days.

(For those of you who have not been concentrating, and who could blame you, we are back to the main bit of the alleged narrative now. You know this when the central character starts to narrate, signified by the use of the word "I". Clever stuff, eh?)

It was during this time that I realised how fortunate I was to have an inside toilet and a well stocked freezer. I was, to put no fine a point on it, frightened. Well, not just frightened but terrified, rather. Or rather terrified. Or maybe just terribly frightened. Anyway, I was having no trouble with my bowel movements, and let's leave it at that.

My nerves were so tight I jumped every time one snapped.

I had seen the terror at first hand on more than one occasion. This alone frightened me and terrified me at the same time. But what was worse, much worse, was realising that I had seen the terror and nobody else had. And nobody else would be willing to believe me. I was alone on the precipice of disaster, a disaster that could rip through the country and the world and no-one would listen. Of course, I hadn't tried to tell anyone about it yet, but that was hardly the point.

I was living in fear. Okay, so technically, I was living in Knaresborough, really, but I was speaking figuratively, which is a tricky thing to master at the best of times and this wasn't the best of times. The fear was the fear of the evil of the ducks.

"My god," I thought to myself as I sat in my comfortable living room armchair thinking about myself thinking in my comfortable living room armchair.

"My god."

I often repeated myself like that.

One policeman and one dog, though not necessarily in that order, had been mercilessly killed at the bills of the devil's beasts... and who knows how many more? Oh, that Irish guy. But would anyone believe the danger they were in? No, was the resounding feeling I had.

Suddenly, the news blurted out from the small black and white portable television which was my one extravagance in my flat. I was almost unconscious to it all as my mind tossed and turned the events of the past days through my troubled thoughts, knotting my brain in my head like a large knot that it would be difficult to unknot without a large unknotting machine. Then I heard it.

"And today in the North Yorkshire town of Knaresborough..."

My ears pricked up, my mind clicked and I fell off my armchair. I was looking at the ceiling.

"...a policeman was killed in a fluke accident involving an escaping convict, a drain cover and the River Nidd. Detectives have found the open drain and are looking into it..."

The fools, the bloody fools, I thought as I lay on the floor. They've missed the truth, they have missed the truth, they have jumped to the wrong conclusions. It wasn't a freak incident, it was the ducks, the ducks, the ducks who murdered him.

Didn't they see? Or was it a cover up? Did they really know and had they decided to submerge the truth? Maybe that was the ploy. Stop a widespread panic, keep the news suppressed, keep us in the dark. Conspiracy theory again.

No. I thought about this. They were probably just being stupid.

"That is the end of the news and now over to Fiona Cunningham with the weather."

"Good evening," smiled Fiona, "and, indeed, it should be for all of us, unless you are unfortunate enough to live in the North. But then again, you don't really count. Tomorrow will be fine and clear in all sunny Southern districts with high temperatures and clear skies. But in the North it will be dark, damp and dismal, especially in Knaresborough where large dark objects will appear menacingly in the black foreboding sky. So, it's goodnight from me."

I switched the television off and quaked. There, for the entire world to see, was the truth, the pointers, the hints, the signs that would be ignored. The lightening cracked and the rumbling began. Yes, so, the weather woman was wrong again. Nothing new there.

I went to the kitchen to make myself something to eat. I avoided the eggs.

I stared out of my window into the dark, foreboding night, listening to the rain slam against the glass and the wind whistle through the curtains. There was a flapping sound that did not fit in with normal meteorological happenings which I chose to ignore. I peeled my potato slowly. I heard another flap that turned into a strange slallop. It seemed to be coming from the hall. I stopped peeling. The slallop happened again. The hall door creaked slowly open. Another slallop.

I stopped breathing. Holding up the potato peeler in my hand, I edged to the hall.

Slallop, slallop, slallop, went the sound.

I held the peeler in the ready position, hoping against hope that whatever was coming into my hall had a skin I could easily peel if required. But what was it that made such a strange watery, fleshy sound when it walked? What went slallop? What did that sound remind me of?

And then I realised. Slallop. Webbed feet. Was it a duck?

I edged to the wall and tightened my grip of my peeler, my hand sweating, my pulse racing, my heart trembling and my bowels in broad sympathy with my entire body. This was it. I breathed in, closed my eyes and dived out into the hall.

"Aaargh!" I cried, a blood curdling yell which actually curdled my blood.

I opened my eyes.

I saw nothing in the hall save for a small pool of water. I held my peeler in front of me, trembling. My breaths panted frantically, whatever that means.

"Sorry, but is that a Snodgrass Peeler or just a normal Tonsmiths one?" asked a voice behind me.

"Waarghhhh!" I replied, thoughtfully.

I jumped up and fell over into the pool of water.

"Sorry," said the voice, "I didn't mean to frighten you."

I turned to see a wet, very wet one-armed man in an ill-fitting safari jacket which dripped constantly onto my hall carpet. He was noticeably bald, save for two crops of greying ginger hair on either side of his head and a large scar on the top of his head.

"Is that peeler loaded, by the way?" he asked.

"Erm, w-what?" I stuttered in reply.

"I've startled you, I can tell, haven't I?" he continued.

"Erm I, what..." I responded articulately.

"It's dripping."

"So are you."

"Oh, yes. It's a little damp out there, you know. Bad night."

The man walked into my room and sat down on my settee, oblivious to his exceeding dampness and its affect on my furniture. He sighed deeply and sank his head into his hand.

"Sorry," he said, looking up. "But you look somewhat surprised to see me."

I non-verbally communicated a look of surprise which he seemed to understand.

"Why?"

I found this difficult to answer. I mean, there was his ability to get through my locked door, the fact I didn't know him from Adam, the unremitting wetness of him, the fact that he didn't look surprised at my surprise and found my astonishment and fear astonishing.

"Erm, oh, no reason," I heard myself responding. "Cup of tea perhaps?"

"Oh, no, look don't put yourself to any trouble, I mean, it looks as though you have potatoes to peel and things. But if you're making one..."

And with that he sank his head into his hand again.

There was a long silence. So I went to make some tea.

From the kitchen, I could hear the low dark murmuring of the man, who occasionally was heard to say something about "...this damn arm..." and "...damn, damn, damn..." and "...damn this damned arm and the one that is no longer here..."

"Erm, sugar?"

"Yes, please."

"One or two?"

"Just one... just this damned one!" he screamed back. "Oh, sorry. Two, please. Large ones."

I brought in the tea and poured. He still dripped onto the settee. I kept quiet for a time, as he did. Then he spoke.

"Sorry. This is obviously not twenty seven, is it?"

"Erm, no, it's not. It's twenty two. But an easy mistake to make, people are making the same mistake all of the time."

"Sorry. I apologise. I heartily apologise. I thought it was twenty seven. I suppose I've got a bit of explaining to do, haven't I? Bursting in here, dripping with water, moaning about my damned arm, saying damn a lot, asking for two large sugars and all..."

"Well, it has been a bit of a surprise," I replied. "But look on the bright side. I mean, I haven't seen anybody for a few days and the settee could do with a bit of a clean..."

"Aargh!" he replied, obviously in pain. "Sorry, this damned arm," he explained, looking at where his arm wasn't.

I avoided eye or arm contact.

As he apologised he yanked a packet of crisps from his safari jacket pocket, pulled them open with his teeth and gulped them all down, almost in one. He'd obviously done *that* before.

He coughed a little and looked at me in the eye.

"Sorry. Only way to kill the pain. Tried everything but only Prawn and Vinegar crisps work. Don't ask me why. Though there are many things unexplained in this world and this is just one of them."

He visibly relaxed as he talked and the crisps he ingested obviously worked.

"Can I explain myself?" he asked. I nodded. "Well, it's like this. I... *aargh*!"

He ate some more crisps.

"Taste so bloody vile that you forget the pain, you see," he explained. "Got it in Africa, or rather lost it there. I was on the trail of... the devil. Do you believe in the devil?"

"Oh, er, well, yes, I suppose... more tea?"

"The devil is there and I had to track it down, but the devil is an evil thing and takes no prisoners. Evil is all around and it will take your arm. But I won. I paid the price but I won. Took me many years but I tracked it down and got it. Got it good. Single handed."

"Single handed?"

He looked at his missing arm, if you can actually do that.

"So to speak. But I paid the price. It was worth it to see the back of the devil... his best side!"

He laughed a little but not much.

"Erm, the devil?" I enquired.

"Yes, the devil. Not as you would think, oh no. No cloven hooves, no red dress, no horns, but, nevertheless, the devil. A devil in the form that you or I would not expect, but that's the trick the devil plays and plays so well. Actually, his best trick was one with a pack of cards and the banana that had us all fooled but he is used to playing tricks. And the greatest trick he ever played was making us not realise that the true devil isn't what we think it may be but instead it is... a duck."

I fell off the armchair.

"You are surprised at that?" he asked.

"No, it's just that I'm not good at sitting in armchairs, I fall off quite regularly," I responded.

He looked at me and, with a flash of lightening lighting the room in a dramatic manner, he realised he had found a soul mate. And then his eyes darkened.

"Oh, no..." he grumbled. "I see in your eyes that the devil has returned. Oh, no, oh, no," he howled, like a dying dog, pained and rather upset.

"More tea?" I asked, pathetically as I quavered in fear at the future.

"No thanks," he replied through the howling. "But have you got any more Prawn and Vinegar crisps?"

She moved her hand onto the screen. Her father had told her not to do that but he was upstairs, asleep.

She moved her palm over the screen, the static making her giggle. She was only three, she was alone in the lounge and it was three o'clock in the morning. She giggled again, a warm, happy giggle.

"They're here," she said as she felt a presence.

A cold shiver ran up her spine.

The television crackled a little and a vision came on the screen.

She smiled at the company.

"They're here."

She had been a problem child. Loved by her parents, adored by her two elder brothers, she had long, blonde hair and an impish grin that smiled out from her dimpled cheeks. She was fun but she did insist on telling people that she could commune with people from other worlds, that she

heard dead people and that she knew what the people across the road were watching on their television. The latter bit was easier than the two former bits, of course, since she got binoculars for her third birthday.

Her parents had taken her to see specialists and doctors but nobody could explain her ability to be a very irritating and a little scary whilst also rather cute. Most said she'd grow out of it if her parents lavished money on her and spoiled her. They decided against this because they were very poor.

She was good at nursery school. Very bright at adding up, she had already started to read and she precociously played the piano to shouts of "Hey, Mozart's at home!" as she tinkled out one of his more obscure piano pieces, so obscure, indeed, that even Mozart may not recognize it.

She knew she had a gift but she wasn't sure what it was yet. She just knew she liked to commune and who could blame her? And that night, she decided that the television was her means of communication, so she sat in front of it, waiting for a message. It was not long in coming.

She turned quickly as she felt the draught.

They were here.

Two of them. Right behind her. Wet webs on the carpet.

They were there and, in an instant, they weren't again. They had done their job.

The television crackled off.

She wouldn't be playing the piano again.

It was a bright sunny day in Richmond and her company, well, government quango thing, had sent her on a fact-finding mission to study traffic calming measures in the small bustling town, probably to get her out of the office. This task mostly seemed to consist of eating ice-cream and staring at the cars and lorries which occasionally passed her or stopping to look at interior design shops and the one shop that specialized in Genealogy in the town, which was unsurprisingly quiet.

As she walked absent mindedly along the main road in the shadow of the castle, there was, indeed, a shadow above and, before she knew it, her large 99 ice-cream was speckled with something from above. She was about to look up when she felt more speckles, then larger droppings, on her shoulder and then a large plop of something smelly and foul on her head.

"Yeuch!" she cried and looked to the skies where she spied a small flock of young ducks, quacking and winking to themselves and mouthing "Dude!" to each other.

Not killers these, just playful conscientious objectors who wanted to do their part for world domination or, in this case, world defecation.

FIVE

"Walt Burnstein? Why, yes, he's a ringer here," said Mrs. Artic down the phone that connected her to the Head Ranger at the Killington Wildfowl Reserve.

"Well, how do you expect me to know where he is? I'm not his mother, after all, although we are distantly related, which is just one of those unfortunate things and not something I am particularly proud of.""

There was a slight silence.

"Well, yes, I do believe that his immediate superior is somebody called Brownie, but that isn't... well, thank *you* too, Mr. North."

Mrs. Artic carefully replaced the phone and gave it a withering look, which she hoped would be felt at the other end of the phone, which it invariably would not have done on grisly old Mr. North, eccentric and especially un-likeable owner of the Wildfowl Reserve. She was insulted at the insinuations. After all, how could she know the exact location of each Ringer at the Reserve? There were up to twenty five at any one time and each had at least an area of twelve square miles to patrol. None were in radio contact, indeed some had a very tenuous contact with the world in general, and few ever appeared at the Control Hut which Mrs. Artic manned (or *"personed"*, as she preferred to call it), even though their conditions of employment made this compulsory.

Walt was one of the more eccentric of the Ringers, which is like saying that Hitler was one of the more ambitious people you've ever met; the local constabulary had arrested him many times under suspicion of "anti social activities near the public areas", whatever that meant, though Mrs. Artic had a few ideas having once had a cocoa with Walt when she had to slap his face when he sat a little too close.

She had no idea if the constabulary's concern was warranted, she only knew that it would certainly explain a thing or two if it was.

She tutted to herself at the memory.

The old wooden door of the Control Hut creaked slowly open. As old wooden doors do.

"Erm," said the ashen face of a policemen as it poked itself around the door. "Erm, I think I've got some bad news for you regarding a Mr. Walt Burnstein, whom I believe is employed here?"

"Depends what the news is this time," replied Mrs. Artic. "Flashing again?"

"Pardon?" said the policemen, blushing a little and looking down to check his flies.

"Walt. Have you caught him flashing?"

"Oh, no, no, no. It's worse than that. In the nets. Covered in blood and feathers. Found him at first light this morning. He's dead, I'm afraid."

"Oh."

Mrs. Artic found it difficult to articulate her indifference in any other way.

"I just need some detail. I believe he worked here on a regular basis?"

"Yes."

"What was his position?"

"He was a Ringer."

"Oh. Well now he's a dead Ringer."

My visitor spent the night in frantic ramifications. I spent it on top of my duvet, sleeping soundly if somewhat uncomfortably, trying to keep his incessant babblings out of earshot, a difficult thing to do as he babbled all night whilst eating forty three bags of crisps, which he had purchased for his "ultimate journey", as he kept calling it.

He had also bought an automatic crisp opener, which just shows you what you can get in the Twenty First Century thanks to the burdening power of Capitalism and the sovereignty of the consumer.

"Help! Help!"

The scream came from a well dressed woman in a long black overcoat on the streets of New York. The policeman was there in no time.

"How can I help you, ma'am?" he asked, looking a little confused as he could see no reason for the screaming.

"A duck! A duck!" she screamed and pointed to a mallard.

"Ma'am, could you desist with the screaming? It's rather *piercing*," asked the policeman, almost politely.

"But the duck..." the woman continued, piercingly.

"Yes, it is a duck, ma'am, so just let him be and he'll let you be, as is the way of the world here in New York.," the policeman responded, calmly.

"The way of the world? But they're killers, killers, they hate human beings and will kill us all!" she responded.

"Ma'am, are you on some sort of substance?" asked the policeman, incredulously, as she didn't look like a substance user.

"No, I am not! I may sue."

"Sorry, ma'am, but you are over reacting to a duck."

"Over-reacting? Do you not know what is going on elsewhere in the world?"

"Erm, I'm American ma'am so the answer to that question is, no. A categorical no."

And with that she started to scream again. Before the policeman could ask her to stop, from the skies came a plethora of superheroes: Spiderman, Superman, Daredevil, The Fantastic Four, Batman and many other that we can't actually name for copyright reasons ('nuff said). As they landed they all looked at each other and wondered who's turn it was to save the world.

"It's actually my day off," explained Superman.

And then from the sky came a second wave of superheroes. Dry Cleaning Man, Half a Head Boy, Defrag Man, Woolly Hat Dog, Trouser Girl, Unicycle Person, Health & Safety Guy and Over-Charged at the Checkout Boy, to name but a few. Oh, and Pull Out Man.

"Oh, you big league guys, how do you always get here first?" asked Defrag Man.

"Contacts," said Spiderman, tapping his nose.

"And intuition," added Daredevil.

"I rely on the bat-phone some days," said Batman, smiling, "and Alfred."

"Well, are you just going to talk or are you going to help me?" asked the woman.

"Why, ma'am, what seems to be the problem?" asked Batman somewhat curtly.

"The duck!" she said pointing. They all looked. But the duck had gone.

They all looked at each other. They shrugged.

"Well, no lives to save here," said all four of the Fantastic Four in unison.

And with that they all bid her farewell and flew back to their super hero lives, all save for Unicycle Person, who was still having problems getting onto his unicycle due to a recent hernia operation that he didn't like to talk about.

"You got a license for that by the way?" asked the policeman as the woman walked away.

Somewhere in Central Park, a vagrant tramped over to a small duck and tried to feed it.

It snapped onto his neck and killed him instantly. And nobody in America noticed.

I awoke early with a start. I could feel a cold sweat on me as I smelt the foul odour of ducks around my body and my environment once again. I kept my eyes tight shut, trying not to quake, struck by and smelling terror. Duck, I thought, but I couldn't.

I had to think quickly. If I truly was cornered in my own bedroom, I had little or no chance, These devil ducks would not take me in my sleep; they enjoyed the thrill of the chase, the fear of their quarry, the look of helplessness in their prey. They would wait for my eyes to open before doing what they did best to me. I smelt the air. I felt surrounded by ducks. Of course, I couldn't see them, but I didn't have to... I knew they were there and I was surrounded, I could feel them, I could sense them, I could smell them.

This was it. If I opened my eyes, I was dead. My sweat ran cold down my face.

The door smashed suddenly open.

There was a voice.

"Open your eyes! That's not duck you can smell! It's my feet!"

"What?" I cried as I leaped up, to see my visitor standing at the foot of my bed with one naked foot in the air, wafting it around and smelling distinctly of rancid duck, if ducks can actually smell rancid.

"Oh, of course," I said, sheepishly. "Would you like breakfast? And can you possibly put some clothes on?"

Over breakfast, I asked this man what his name was.

"I don't know yours," he said, which was correct but, let's face it, I'd asked first.

"Look..." I said.

"I knew you'd say that."

"What?"

"What you will say next."

"You mean..?"

"Yes."

"But..."

"Don't."

"Don't what!"

"You know."

"Will you stop..."

"Anticipating what you are going to say? It's not anticipation, John, it's..."

"E.S.P.... must be catching."

"It's deeper than E.S.P., John. It's Ultra Sensory Enhanced Lisionary and Elongated Special Senses," he said, without a blink of the eyes.

"USELESS?" I asked.

"No, it can come in handy at times. You see, I was given this curse due to a rather unfortunate accident when I was two. Luckily, I'm only one now. Psychiatry is a wonderful thing, John."

"By the way," I interrupted, "my name isn't John."

"No problem. My senses aren't always right... but they do sense the presence of... ducks," he said with a dramatic... *pause*.

I shivered. I almost choked on my grapefruit. Only the fact that I wasn't eating grapefruit saved me. How did he know? Where did he come from? Why was he eating my grapefruit?

"How do I know?" he asked, knowingly. "You know, you sometimes just know. I can smell them. I am used to their smell; you have to be when you have spent three months on your knees tracking the little devils, desperate to nail them, to catch them, to destroy their evil for ever. We are, as I think you know, in mortal danger from these, these beasts, which is why I tracked them for three months, three whole months!"

I was in awe. "Three whole months?"

"Yes. It would have been just three days had I not have mistaken a diesel tanker that had run into a duck pond in Huddersfield but that's where your enhanced senses can let you down. A natural mistake to make, really."

I got my grapefruit and ate it in trepidation rather than the breakfast room, as normal. I could only sit and gaze at this strange yet fascinating man in front of me who seemed to share my knowledge and fear of ducks as well as my liking for grapefruit for breakfast. Yet mixed with fear was a feeling of relief that somebody else knew, somebody else understood, somebody else cared, even if they were a messy eater.

He stopped eating, dramatically, and looked at me.

"We must do something and there is only one thing to do," he said. "We must... seek help."

This somewhat disheartened me after the last paragraph.

"But where, you are going to ask," he interrupted my thoughts, again, which was starting to be a little annoying to say the least. "Well..."

"I wasn't going to ask that!" I tried to say.

"No matter. We must go to Halami Butunque, a small village in the eastern edge of deepest Africa where we will seek the advice and support of the only people who can possibly defend the human race against these devils, against their tide of wickedness, against the terrible power of their evil! We need help for these ducks are not human!"

He was waving his arm about at this stage in a frenzy of activity, emphasising his point. Unfortunately, this arm was attached to his grapefruit by the grapefruit spoon... but not for long. The grapefruit flew through the air and crashed into my newly washed window. With a bit of a bang and a slurp.

"Oh, sorry," he said. "Didn't mean that. But I knew it was going to happen. Erm where was I?"

"The ducks aren't, erm, human."

"Oh, yes. They are not human! They are dangerous, evil beings, spawned of the devil himself, inflicting their ways on the human race, interested in carnage and death, but not always in that order, dedicated to the destruction of mankind. The
human race cannot hope to survive whilst these beasts have it in their mind to overrun us... unless, unless..."

He stopped, quaking, shaking, quivering, his face a bright crimson, bubbling with fear, rage, anxiety and just a touch of amateur acting. But in his speech he had told me of the power of these ducks, their threat and how close I had come to death on two occasions now, occasions that were only a small symptom of the total malaise which faced us all. And then there was a ring at the door. It was the milkman.

"You're behind again, you are," he told me. "Three weeks behind, you get right up my nose, havin' to come here every week and gettin' nowt for my troubles." He seemed to be wavering between a very poor Cockney accent into an even poorer Yorkshire one with each syllable. "That's eight quid you is owin' me, like, me old cock sparrer, ain't it, like, luv."

I had to admit that this mercenary demand paled into insignificance when compared to the world-wide threat of the ducks. The wavering accent didn't help his cause, either.

"Why are you wearing Wellington boots?" I asked, once I'd noticed that he was.

"Ay? You what, luv, like, guvnor? Now, don't you start to play slippery wiv me, mate, my bruvver knows a few guys who it ain't pretty to mess with, if you get my drift, squire, like," he replied, touching the side of his nose with a milk bottle.

"Erm, the ducks," I responded.

"Hey? What?" he asked, pushing his hat back over his head. "Ducks?"

"Yes, erm, d-ducks."

This did not seem to be an acceptable excuse.

"Look, me old cock sparrer," he said, his face scrunching incredulously at me, "you may be around the twist but you owe me money, see, and I want it and I want it now, the money, that is, just in case that last comment was open to misinterpretation, if you get my drift."

"Ducks."

I was getting a little predictable in my responses now.

The milkman was silent for a while. But not for long.

"Okay, okay, I've been as patient as a milkman can be and I ain't gonna be patient no more," And he wasn't; he picked me up by my pajamas and lifted me up the wall. "Ducks, is it. Well, duck this for starters..."

"My dear man," interrupted my one-armed interloper, somewhat fortuitously, to my mind, "may I ask exactly what you are doing?"

"Who's a dis?" asked the milkman, flopping into Italian gangster mode by this time.

"My name is not important," replied the man who's name obviously is not important, "but you do not realise what you have stepped into here. You have stumbled into the midst of a national emergency where milk based financial matters pale into insignificance given the level of threat which we all currently face."

The milkman didn't drop me but looked momentarily confused.

"Has he swallowed a bloomin' dictionary, or what?" he asked. "Look, squire, I is only after what is legally mine, that's all, just after me dosh."

"Yes," replied my visitor, quietly yet firmly, "I understand but you must understand that, as we argue here on John's doorstep, that you are in grave danger from the shadow of a winged terror which inhabits the surrounding skies in numbers un-thought of by mere mortals like yourself. In such circumstances, money is no cushion, no defence and no support."

"You try tellin' that to me trouble and strife, mate," replied the (now Cockney) milkman.

"I do not need to tell her for she will shortly know."

And, at that moment, the milkman's mobile phone rang. He let me slip to the floor and answered the phone. Without hearing the message, we knew what had happened. The milkman looked at us in fear.

"And don't go near your float!" called my new friend as the milkman, eyes wide open, rushed down the stairs, shouting as he ran.

But, to no avail. We ran to the window to see the milk float screech off into the road... with three mallards amongst the gold tops and orange juice. The three ducks looked up to us, behind the safety of our net curtain, and I swear they smiled at us.

The float turned the corner. There was a long, deafening silence. And then a blood curdling crash, followed once more by silence only interrupted by the buzzing of the morning street lamps.

"No, no!" I bellowed.

But it was too late. All we could do now was stand and listen to the silence of the lamps. The ducks had claimed another victim.

The detective entered the cold clinical room with trepidation.

"You can't bring that dog in here," said the man in the white coat, "even if he is a police dog and he is called Trepidation."

The detective apologised and left the dog outside. He explained to the white coated man who he was and why he was there.

"Ah, those ducks, detective!" said the white coated man.

"Yes, but is it ducks? Or just duck?" said the detective, enigmatically. "Is it, indeed, a duck at all?" he asked. "Or maybe a front for another sort of killer? Or maybe it isn't murder at all?"

"You ask a lot of questions," said the white coated man.

"It's my job to be inquisitive," explained the detective, "I'm a detective."

The white coated man smiled and took the detective from the cold clinical ante-room through to his large, tiled room where he did things to dead bodies, the room with the bright fluorescent white lights which lit up the slab, standing dramatically in the centre of the room with nothing else around it, wasting loads of space and being a real nightmare to heat, on which lay the body of a recent victim. The detective pulled back the white cloth and winced.

"Yes, sorry, that's my lunch," said the white coated man.

"Are you on a diet?" asked the detective.

"Yes. Does that make me a suspect?"

"No, just a little overweight. Anyway, is this the man?"

"Woman."

"Blimey. Those ducks are vicious."

"If it is a duck. You said…"

"It's my job to be inquisitive, professor, yours simply to provide me with the facts."

"What, like Cardinal Richelieu died in 1842?"

"No, about the body and what you think caused the death."

There was a long silence. Then the white coated man spoke again.

"Of Cardinal Richelieu?"

"No, not of Cardinal Richelieu. As I said, I need the facts so please keep to the facts. What do you know? About this body, by the way, just in case you get back to the Cardinal."

And he took out his pad, flipped to an empty page and licked his pen.

"Sorry," he said, "I thought I had a pencil. My tongue will be blue for weeks now. Tastes horrible. Anyway, professor, the facts."

And he gave the white coated man a stern stare.

The white coated man took the stare, pulled back the cloth and started to point out lesions, cuts, bites, scrapes and a small nibble on the back of the left ear. He suggested that the woman was attacked by somebody or something just twenty hours ago. He further suggested that she had died of a heart attack due to the fury of the attack and maybe the shock of being attacked from the rear. There were forty to fifty marks on the body itself. The cuts and lesions were not made by a weapon, well, not in the way we would normally mean " a weapon". The marks were consistent with a beak like shape. He further explained that all of this, save for the nibble on the ear, pointed to a duck or a duck like animal.

"A duck *like* animal?"

"Yes. I can't believe that a normal duck would do this to a human being. After all, they are not meat eaters."

"Professor, I may not know much but I know that human beings are meat eaters," corrected the detective.

"I meant ducks are not meat eaters. Ducks like to swim in water and put their heads under the water to get food, for example, they will eat tadpoles, small frogs, small fish and water snails. Which is not nice but the way they are. It's dog eat dog in the animal kingdom, though not literally speaking. Ducks also like to mix water with their food, because it makes the food softer and easier to swallow, plus they can spit it further if needs be. Ducks can also mate in water."

The detective pointed out he didn't need to know this.

"Oh, yes, sorry, getting carried away there. Anyway, if ducks are kept in a house, putting the food and water side by side is best. Then the ducks can eat some food and then drink a little water with the food. If the food and water are put in places far apart, then the ducks have to run from one place to the other to eat. That is how they survive. Seldom, when in a house, will they decide to kill a human being."

"But the facts in front of us suggest otherwise, professor," corrected the detective.

The white coated man scratched his chin.

"Yes, you have a point. It is strange, as ducks are usually very timid and nervous animals; they are easily upset by sudden changes in their environment, such as, say, the sudden appearance of a dog, another domesticated animal or a human being, unless the human being has bread crusts in a bag, of course. Indeed, even the appearance of a sudden light at night can upset them. Sudden changes such as these may cause ducks to lose some of their feathers in a moult in extreme cases. Ducks are easily hurt by domesticated animals such as dogs because they cannot run as fast and cannot fight them."

"Yet they allegedly killed a dog," the detective pointed out.

The white coated man scratched his chin.

"Yes," he seemed to agree, "very strange behaviour and not a behaviour I would expect from a normal duck or related species. Yes, we know that some ducks can be, shall we say, aggressive at times. Breeds such as the Pekin and Muscovy,
whilst rare in these isles, are very fast growers and have been known to reach up to three feet in height and be able to hold their own in a fight. However, they have hardly ever been known to show the aggressive tendencies connected with homicidal attacks as we may have here. Though, detective, do you know that the Muscovy duck is the only breed that can fly up into trees for roosting at night?"

"No, no, I didn't know that. But isn't that irrelevant?"

"No, that's a big thing with a trunk."

There was a short silence.

"So, I have to admit to being confused," continued the white coated man. "I know my ducks, detective, as I have probably shown you. Whilst this looks like a duck attack yet we have hardly ever seen such behaviour in a duck."

"Ah, *hardly* ever? You said *hardly* ever, professor."

The white coated man scratched his chin yet again. And nodded.

"Yes, *hardly* ever," he repeated with *emphasis*. "A colleague of mine has done some research to suggest that this is not, historically, an isolated incident. We poo-poohed her theory, mainly because she is very attractive and we all feel rather geeky and impotent in her company, as she is not only very clever and extremely good looking but has exceptional inter-personal skills, unlike the rest of her peers. She also has a great pair of legs. Her significant research seems to suggest that a new breed, a strange subset of the species, has found its way to this country and may have nested somewhere in Yorkshire. The first reported incidents she found were many years back and were once recorded in the books of Sir Darrington Womersley but little factual evidence remains. His books were destroyed, we believe, by people who were afraid of his suggestion that ducks were not always playful, comical beasts but, in fact, descendents of the devil. Sir Darrington Womersley was himself killed in exceedingly suspicious circumstances at the great lake on his own estate. People prefer not to speak of him now. So, the concept of the killer duck was mostly thought to be myth and superstition, stories passed down from generation to generation, a devil duck being a good way of frightening the kids and making sure that they brushed their teeth and said their prayers at night, but her research suggests that this is not true; the beast really did exist. And maybe still exists."

"I don't deal with myths I only deal in facts," the detective stereotypically said. "So, do you have her number?"

The white coated man blushed.

"I wish," he mumbled.

"No, I mean..."

"Oh, sorry, yes, but no."

"Her name then?"

"Erm, no. All I know is that she is on her way to Holland to report her findings. She's got auburn hair, if that helps?"

The detective chewed on his pen again.

"Not really but you have been a help, professor. I thank you for your time. Now, I must be going. I need to wash this ink off my tongue"

The white coated man stopped him as he made his exit.

"So, detective, what do you think? Are these ducks really a threat to our very existence?"

The detective scratched his chin.

"No, not really."

"Should we be frightened?"

"Yes, I think so," said the detective, enigmatically, and he let himself out, collecting Trepidation on the way.

The white coated man scratched his chin again. And got back to his decorating.

SIX

He never thought he could be so much in love. Totally, utterly, head over heels in love. And not just with her but with the entire campus of the University, the city the University was in, the wonderful county of Yorkshire it was in and the North of England itself! It was love!

"The North of England!"

He smiled, inwardly and outwardly, as he said it to himself. But how strange. Just a month or so ago, he was in abject misery as he realised that his dream of an education at the dreamy Oxbridge spires had been shattered and that he would have to get used to the idea of an education in a grimy Northern red-brick affair, where all people wore clogs and talked in strange, almost indecipherable accents. But now, now... despite his intellectual upbringing in the frantic charm of the big city, he had now been wooed by the uncluttered, rustic charm of this cold, dark yet ostensibly welcoming Northern city. And they didn't *all* wear clogs!

Wooed, charmed, seduced and finally bedded in the shape of a slender, blonde haired Northern nymph from Cleckheaton, whom he had met at the Fresher's Disco the night before. It had certainly been an interesting twenty four hours!

The sun was barely rising over the drooping oaks as Andrew shuffled along the gravel path which led away from the girls' hall of residence, back towards Livingstone House at the opposite end of the campus. Andrew softly mumbled her name to himself, noticing little behind the thick silver frames of his glasses. He didn't need to notice much; he was in love. Deeply in love. Even at that time of the morning. And this time it was forever, again.

His weak chin fell, insignificantly, under the size of his mumbling and all embracing smile.

"Ethel, Ethel, oh how I love you, Ethel," he repeated to himself, slowly, constantly as he walked along, oblivious to the sun, the morning mist, the early traffic and the ducks at the side of the campus pond.

The early traffic ignored him.

"Ethel... um, I wonder what Phillippa would think now?" he thought, zipping up his green Parker jacket.

Phillippa was Andrew's fiancée. He had bid a tearful farewell to her just yesterday at Kings Cross, promising to phone her that evening to talk about their love, children, detached houses and private education. He'd forgotten to phone. Well, he'd been drinking a little. And he wasn't missing her. After all, she was about 220 miles away and looking forward to her morning battle with the underground crowds by now and it is, after all, possible to love two different people with the same intensity, as long as it's only you who does the loving, especially when this was the real thing, or something close to it. He could tell that; they'd know one another for, oh, almost eight hours now and he was sure of it. Even if half of that time was spent asleep.

Andrew rubbed his neck and mused upon the hardness of campus floors. Still, it was the North. The North of England! Oh how he loved the sound of that now!

He crossed the bridge over the University pond and passed a young girl, clutching an armful of Media Study files and the yearning in his loins yearned once more. It is, after all, possible to love *three* people at once, isn't it?

As he stopped and admired the view, the two pochards below looked up. Andrew stopped. Looking down at them, he chose to ignore their presence. He knew little of wildlife, save for the porcelain doves he had given Phillippa for her eighteenth birthday last week, a sign of his undying love. He knew what doves were; he couldn't tell a pochard if it came up to him and ripped his throat apart. Which was a pity for this was exactly what was about to happen.

Just as he smiled that sickly loving smile, to be exact.

A dull thump was all that disturbed the early morning mist as his body rolled into the pond, to be dragged into the rushes by the two pochards. All that remained of Andrew was an unused pack of contraceptives. And his grin.

He never did tell me his name and I felt I didn't have to ask him for it. I was quite happy with my own and I trusted him intrinsically as one you could trust with your own life, one you would turn to in an emergency, one who could handle any situation single-handed, which was pretty fortunate when you remembered that he did only have one hand. Which he did a good job of opening a packet of crisps with.

After we had witnessed, helplessly but luckily off-screen, the horrific end of the milkman, he looked at me in silence for a moment and then muttered something in Arabic. I was stunned; I hadn't heard Arabic spoken so well since I was a four year old, indeed, I hadn't heard it spoken too well then as I was born and brought up in Cheltenham which did not have an indigenous Arabic population.

I could tell, though, that his utterances had substance and depth. It was as if another force had overtaken his body, spoken as they were in a grim monotone.

"Do you see what I mean?" he asked.

"Well, most of it apart from the Arabic bits," I replied.

"So, you knew it was Arabic?" he asked.

"It was a guess, really. So what does it mean?"

"Why don't you guess?" he replied, somewhat sarcastically.

"Could it be that the ducks are hell-bent on world domination, which they only feel can be achieved by the total annihilation of the human race as they are not too good at communication, negotiation and compromise?"

He was silent. He scratched his chin.

"Erm could be," he replied, somewhat sheepishly this time.

"Could be? What do you mean, could be?" I asked, aghast.

"Well, I haven't the faintest idea, myself. I only did 'O' level French at school. It's just that I occasionally break into this Arabic stuff. Can be quite embarrassing when all you want is to buy a packet of crisps. I wonder what it does mean?"

I sighed with deep disappointment for, in his words, I was hoping for a meaning, an explanation, some sort of understanding of the current situation. But no, not from this stranger now in my house. Or maybe...

"Or then..." he started and then stopped. "No."

Broodingly, he sat for an hour or more, engrossed in thought and the occasional mumble, with odd visits to the toilet, stroking his stubbly chin. The clock ticked noisily in the surrounding quietness, unable to stir him from his awkward thoughts, the dark understandings of a man troubled by the knowledge he had and the frustration of not knowing how to deal with the knowledge he had. Well, if you got an instruction booklet and it was all in Arabic, you'd struggle a bit, wouldn't you? Unless you were Arabic, obviously.

He leapt suddenly from his seat. Now was perhaps the moment of divine enlightenment we had been waiting for.

"Is it Tuesday?" he asked, dramatically.

"No, it's Wednesday, I think," I replied.

"Oh." He sunk back into his chair again. "Well, I was close. I must..." his voice rose again,"... I must... have a shave. Haven't had one since the last time."

And with that he headed off for the bathroom.

I sighed with relief as he left. He returned twenty five minutes later and his balding head was covered in more scars than before.

"Your head?" I asked,

"Gruesome isn't it?" he retorted.

"But, how, erm, did... was it ducks?" I asked, trembling at the thought of the memories that this may elicit and the response I may get.

"Oh, no. I'm just not very good at shaving, that's all."

He smiled, squeezed his crisp packet open and flipped a score of crisps into his mouth. He chewed as his head continued bleeding.

"Look," he said," I've been thinking whilst I was shaving and I think that this duck problem is only starting here. I've seen it before but not as bad. I've encountered these devils before, but, I have to say that this is different. I get a different feel. My Arabic is longer. This time, this time... but why choose here? What is there about... erm, where am I?"

"Knaresborough."

"Where's that, for God's sake?"

"Well, it's a small town in North Yorkshire made famous by its dropping well and the prophesies of Old Mother Shipton," I responded in an attempt to clarify matters for him and any reader who was not used to Yorkshire and its environs.

"Old Mother Shipton?" he asked, incredulously.

"Yes." I looked for divine interpretation and a flash of illuminated explanation.

"Oh, never heard of her. So, why here, why now? I think that it's only going to get worse. It's the start of something, I can tell. At the moment it's a small town in North Yorkshire made famous by its dropping well and the prophecies of some old bint I've never heard of but soon it could be the world. Of course, the authorities, fools that they are, will never believe that a few mindless murders are only the presage to world domination by a species of animal that we have previously only seen as mostly submissive."

"Are you sure?" I asked.

"Oh, yes. The authorities never listen to such panic talk."

"No, not about that. I mean, I thought ducks were a species of bird, surely, not animal."

"Are you sure? Animals, I'd have thought or maybe insects. But birds? No, not birds, are they?"

"I think you'll find..."

"Well, I'll look it up on my way to the authorities. Where I'm not going, of course, 'cos they won't listen. Blimey... we're in trouble, you know."

This was not the comforting word I was looking for.

"Unless I have the answer," he added, enigmatically. "Which I do. Tell me, how do you stop a weed from taking control of a garden?"

I was dumbfounded by the question.

"Oh, get Mr. Hopground in, you mean?" I asked.

"Eh?" he responded.

"Our gardener, Mr. Hopground. Very good with weeds and especially good with moss. Our lawn this time last year was riddled with..."

He was looking at me sternly with a look that would distil whiskey, if that's how whiskey is distilled.

"Not Mr. Hopground, then?" I added, remorsefully.

"No. It was a hypothetical question."

"Well, it was a hypothetical answer. I mean, I know he's good with moss but I haven't the faintest what he's like with ducks and... I'm prattling again, aren't I?"

His silence told me I was.

"So," he started again, "to kill weeds successfully, you need to get to the roots."

"That's just what Mr. Hopground... erm, carry on."

"So, we must get to the root of this problem. They have chosen Knaresborough, they are here for a reason, they know their aim and the length of their ambition. We do not. So, we need help. No," he interrupted me before I could say it, "not Mr. Hopground, whom I feel may be out of his depth here, but the guru of world threats, the aptly named Andar Am Khasmir of Olligatumur."

"Oh, right," I replied, feigning understanding and wondering if this meant that we'd be headed for Wales soon.

"And we must go before it is... too late."

He liked the dramatic pause but you've probably noticed that yourself by now.

"To the airport!"

Her eyes twinkled and she walked across the departure lounge in a confident manner.

Auburn haired, well dressed, young, slightly tanned and ferociously intelligent, she had sailed through Cambridge gaining first class honours, a Masters and a reputation for being able to take a zambucca or seven. Despite a myriad of offers, she had decided against the attractions of the business world and marriage and instead had gone into the wonderful yet underpaid world of research and being single. Animal research. Duck research, to be accurate. Well, ducks and other wildfowl. She found it fascinating and slightly dangerous, currently. But today she was exhilarated, excited and other such emotions as she walked across to the international check in desks.

She was now on her way to an International Conference on Ornithology in Holland where she was giving a rather left-field presentation entitled "The Psychopathic Tendencies of Ducks and Other Water Fowl in Certain Scenarios" after a short study into some recent behaviour at a wildfowl trust we can't mention due to contractual reasons.

The presentation was going to be very timely.

"Big teeth, killers." She liked that.

And if our heroes had have been earlier arriving at the airport, we could have subtly manufactured a meeting between our narrator and this fine yet intelligent young lady which could well have led to them all saving the day.

She could also have been the much needed love interest in this book but our author realized just how ill-equipped he was to form a fully rounded female character, so he let her quietly slip onto the plane to Amsterdam without bumping into the two main characters.

Which was a great pity. As she did have great legs.

So, in no time at all after having no useful contact with somebody we didn't know at the airport but who ultimately could have helped us whilst adding some love interest into the story, and, let's face it, completely beyond the realms of reality, we set off for Africa, touching down in the remote jungle of Olligatumur (twinned with Bracknell) and striding towards the small village where we were told our saviour lived. This turned out to be a quite inhospitable place which entailed a three day trek through wild jungle and dangerous swamps. We could have got the local bus but he liked to do things the hard way.

We lost all but three of our experienced jungle back packers, or "cabbies", as they were apparently known in this area, not to wild animals but to television crews who were looking to create some sort of documentary about this sort of thing.

Andar Am Whatsisname lived in a tree house in the middle of a clearing off the banks of a tepid river. Not my idea of high society and, let's face it, not a parking spot for miles (the car parks were all full due to a local car boot sale), but at least we had reached our destination and maybe our saviour in our darkest hour. We were shattered after our trek, the flies buzzed and bit around us, we were in desperate need of a bath and sustenance, but we carried on and knocked on the bottom of his tree house, our spirits lifting as we felt our journey coming to an end.

This was the place that spelled salvation to a threatened yet ignorant world.

A face appeared at the top of the tree.

"We've already got one, whatever you're selling," it shouted in a very good English accent.

"What?" my traveling companion replied. "We are not selling anything. We are here for the salvation of the world. We are here to see Andar Am Kashmir."

There was a short silence.

"Oh, yes. He's moved. Try the small bungalow by the airport. He went last week; fed up of the commuting, by all accounts. And it's easier for those who are seeking omnipotent understanding of the reasons for small beasts trying to conquer the human race to get to see him as it's not such a long trek as it has been to this godforsaken hole, though, let's face it, it's home to me, so why should I complain?"

We stood in silence.

"Though the woodpeckers can be a bloody nuisance," the voice needlessly added.

We turned back with a heavy heart. Luckily, we hadn't spent many paragraphs trying to find him. Well, not yet, any way.

So, we now had little answer to this terrible threat to our world and, to add to my torment, we were miles away from my home in Knaresborough, confused, tired and smelling of the jungle, and not the good bits.

What was happening back in England, I mused to myself as I sat in my self pity. By now the ducks could have taken over all of Knaresborough and be on their way to Otley, laying waste the bustling cities of West Yorkshire, killing, murdering, maiming and quacking on their way to world domination. It seemed a strange place to start but, hey, here we were in Africa, of all places, on a wild goose chase, by the looks of things. What were we going to do about it? Nothing, at this rate. I had to tackle my new friend. He lurched into a green lagoon and flapped about.

"What the heck did you do that for?" he asked.

"Erm sorry, I took myself a little too literally," though I did realise that it was a tackle that Chopper Harris would have been proud of, though I would no doubt have been red carded in these modern times.

"Well, get me out of here!" he yelled as our experienced jungle crew downed bags and put a kettle onto the portable gas stove they had brought with them tutting at me and sharing conspiratorial glances at their weird leaders.

"No," I defiantly and somewhat irrationally replied, "no, I won't, at least, not until you tell me what your name is."

"What? My name?"

"Yes, your name."

"But my name, my name, why do you want to know my name? Why is that important?"

There was a little bit of a lull as I gathered my thoughts.

"Oh, yes, your name. Well, look here, you walk into my flat, live off me for a couple of days, borrow £50 off me at the airport for your darned prawn and vinegar crisps..."

"Which are now soaked through!"

"...yes, which are now soaked through, fly me to the other side of the world..."

"Africa."

"...yes, well, Africa, trek me across inhospitable jungle for umpteen days to find a guy who isn't here anymore and, well, I don't even know your name! Isn't that reason enough!!??"

"You're getting a bit tense, aren't you?"

"TENSE! TENSE! Yes, I'm getting a bit tense! Wouldn't you! The very world is at risk, you seem to be the only one who has any sort of answers, I'm in Africa stuck in the middle of a jungle when I didn't even know they had jungles in Africa and I'm stuck with a bloke whose name I don't even know. And I bet I forgot to cancel the milk."

There was a short but deafening silence. The whistle on the kettle whistled.

"Look," said my friend who's name I did not know, "if it will make life easier, I'll give you the £50 back. It's a little bit damp at the moment but..."

"It's not that!"

"Fair enough, I'll consider it a gift then..."

"It's just that I need to know your name. It's a small point, a little bit of detail but it's just something I need to know, okay! Just tell me your name!"

There was a silence. Then he started to talk but, as he did, from the edge of the lagoon came a slow, premeditated flapping that rippled the otherwise still surface of the water, a flapping caused by the evil presence of a... duck! My friend's mouth moved but I could hear nothing, focused as I was on the shape at the side of him, swiveling slowly into my view but oblivious to him, its wings flapping like the wings of an assassin, its bill aimed menacingly at the liver area of the one armed man who stood damply in the lagoon, oblivious to the ultimate threat to his very existence, ready for the kill. It seemed to glide noiselessly, slowly, coldly in the thin warm air, menacing in its speed and silence.

"Duck! Duck!" I instinctively shouted and all of our bag carriers did. But he didn't. He just looked at me, puzzled.

"Duck!" I squealed again.

"How did you know?" were his final words as I leaped into the lagoon and grabbed him, knocking him under the green, rippling water, just in time to divert his body from the murderous intentions of the duck.

I felt the very down of the killing machine brush past me as we were submerged in the green water and surfaced again to see it career into the whistling kettle of the bag carriers, exploding in a mess of hot water and feathers all over our helpers.

I sighed my relief and spat out a mouthful of lagoon water.

His head emerged from the lagoon shortly after mine, the small strands of hair at the side of his head plastered to his round skull and his confused looking face.

"How did you know my name?" he asked, carrying on our conversation as if there had been no interruption.

"I didn't," I replied.

"You do, you shouted it twice, Duck, Duck, you shouted, I heard you!"

"Duck, Duck?"

"No, just Duck, actually, no hyphen."

"But I shouted duck as there was duck behind you. Didn't you notice?"

"No, but I think I'm either starting to sweat a bit too much or I'm very, very wet."

I pointed to the kettle or at least its remains, surrounded as it was now by our confused and rather irritated bag carriers who now knew that they'd now have to go without a cup of tea and tried to explain what had happened but Duck didn't seem to take it all in.

"Look. It was after you. It could have killed you, you could now be a victim" I explained.

"Why, I could have been..."

"Yes."

"And you..."

"Yes, I did."

"I don't know how to..."

"You don't have to, you know, anyone would have."

There was a long, embarrassed, astounded silence as we both sat in the lagoon, dripping.

"They're on to us," said Duck. "They know where I am."

And suddenly I realised what he'd said.

"Duck?" I shouted, astonished at the irony of the name.

And Duck ducked down into the lagoon again.

It was eleven o'clock in the normally busy Yorkshire town but today the streets were bizarrely empty.

The wind whistled lazily, as it always does, around the empty main street, blowing yesterday's newspapers from empty building to empty building as if looking for human beings to be read by. Their search would be a futile one today for today there were no human beings to be found.

Along the main street strutted a duck, followed by another and then another and then another. As a noise rose in an adjoining street they stopped, as one, and looked towards the sound and, as one, flashed off in its direction.

They reached the din and as quickly as it had started so it stopped. Two young ducks battered, unsuccessfully, against the doors of a takeaway burger bar, to no end, quacking frustratingly at their lack of success. The older ducks tutted and quacked and walked away.

America seemed a long way off, not surprisingly, since it was, but why that worried me was a matter for me and not you, dear reader. My mind was going, drifting, floating away like a boat adrift in duck infested waters, affected, no doubt, by the sizzling heat of the African jungle. Like my trousers. Now they had dried they had decided not to shrink but had, instead, enlarged, especially my turn-ups, which were now dragging on the floor, causing me to trip at regular intervals now we had started to trek on once again. Our baggage handlers thought this hilarious; I had found a good use for the revolver Duck had given me "just in case".

Duck was very nervous and jumpy. Every time I fell and they laughed, Duck would shoot his revolver, which he had brought "just in case the just in case isn't just enough."

We were running low on baggage carriers. And my knees hurt.

"I thought it was a hyena," he would say each time he shot.

"A hyena, in Africa?" I laughed, to myself, that is, as it is always dangerous to laugh at a man with a smoking gun.

"Surely you mean *AN* hyena?" corrected Duck.

"Yes, I think you're right," I said, though I felt he was wrong. Why argue with a man with a gun and a very bad attitude?

"Erm, excuse me butting in but, I think you'll find that with a consonant that you very seldom say *AN*, though it can be used as with *an hotel* or even *an handbag*."

This came from one of our remaining baggage carriers, the one who had packed a spare kettle and was now looking rather nervously down the barrel of a smoking revolver. Duck eyed him up.

At that moment, he had a manic, frightening look about him. I had not known him for long but this look was not a good one. I was a little scared both for me and the bag carrier. If he shot another one, I'd be carrying lots of bags.

"You mean to say that you would say *AN* handbag?" he asked slowly and rather menacingly. There was short silence.

"Well, no, probably not, I think, but maybe, in really posh surroundings with pretentious types I might, but only to mock them," came the stumbling reply.

Duck cocked his revolver. I felt for our carrier.

"That's all right then," said Duck un-cocking and putting his revolver away.

I shuffled up to Duck, taking care not to trip over my trousers, and whispered to him. He stopped at the urgency of my question. He looked me deep into my eyes and sighed.

"Yes," he whispered, "I know he's wrong but, hey, if I had to shoot him we'd run out of baggage carriers in no time."

"Good point," I said just before I fell over again.

The publisher looked at him.

"Killer ducks?"

"Why are we having this meeting in a stairwell?" asked the writer.

"Oh, you know, privacy, embarrassment, you know, look, so, Killer Ducks, you say," came the weak reply as he leaned against the banister attempting and failing to look nonchalant.

"Yes," replied the writer, looking down the forty feet to the ground floor below, "it's not supposed to be founded in..."

"Can't you do a Da Vinci Code sort of thing?"

"Well, no," said the author, "I'm not good at that sort of stuff..." as he looked again quizzically down the stairwell which gaped and yawned at him through the stairs.

"Or Jane Austen, or Doctor Who or Jack Whatsisname or something that sells millions? You know, the new Harry Potter? I've got a mortgage to pay, you know."

"Well, yes..."

"... and I doubt if we'd sell more than 71 of the Killer Ducks thing. To be honest with you"

There was an embarrassed silence.

"Is it funny?" he asked, half heartedly.

"Not really."

"Great. Let me think about it. I'll phone you."

"Okay," said the author as he took up his manuscript and left his publisher via the stairwell.

"Killer ducks," tutted the publisher.

The waiting duck struck the author a glancing blow on the head, knocking him over the banister he was being nonchalant on just minutes before, sending him traveling through the air sideways from the stairs, turning over in the air as he went. The publisher fell forty feet and landed on his back across the cement of the ground floor, his head opened and stuff came out and turned red. The duck flew off, never seen again.

The publisher's arms and legs twitched a bit, like a pig's after it had been killed.

The author smiled, rather pathetically, really.

"Pyrrhic but fun," he muttered through his cracked glasses.

Duck was looking very warm.

His manic grin worried me somewhat. Well, a lot. As was his shooting ability or, rather, lack of shooting ability.

I decided that, at present, it would be unwise to antagonize him in any way at all, like disagreeing with him or sneezing in his presence or things like that.

"Want a crisp?" he asked.

I didn't. I could not stand the taste or smell of those foul, ill-tasting crisps which had the texture of dry cardboard with less of the desirability and the taste of dead dog. But I had to humour him. I smiled awkwardly, took a crisp and placed it in my mouth, keeping an inane grin on my face as I did and moving my hand to my mouth to avoid unnecessary wretching. But better to wretch than to be shot by Duck, I rationalized.

He was obviously a man under pressure: the ducks, his poor trouser choice, those crisps, the hat he wasn't wearing. There were many threats to his sanity.

"Almost out of the damn things" he said.

"Bullets?" I asked, hopefully.

"No, crisps. Got enough bullets for a few more bag carriers, should they upset me."

I swallowed hard. Yeuch.

He strode on into the jungle with me as close to him as I could possibly get, as we were down wind.

I was also finding it hard to keep up as not only did I have my baggage to carry but also our baggage carrier, who said his father had always given him piggy backs when he was tired and, anyway, he thought that he was over the allotted ten hours statutory baggage carrying allowed under EU laws.

The heat did not help, nor the trees, nor the taste of crisps, nor the mud nor the singing of the baggage carrier.

"But I like to sing."

Which was a pity.

"And watch out for them..."

Too late. I thought it was the next line in his song but it was a direct warning about the tree that was once just in front of me and which now we were part of.

"Ouch" said the being-carried-bag-carrier. "That hurts."

"Duck!" I pleaded from underneath the weight above, "help!"

Poking my head from the mess, I could see nothing but branches and leaves.

Then from a small shrub, came a slow stirring, followed by the balding, scarred head of our intrepid but obviously annoyed leader.

"Will you please stop saying that!" he screamed, his menacing eyes looking at me even more menacingly than they had lately and they had been pretty high in the menacing stakes of late.

"Saying what?" I asked, somewhat naively.

"My name."

"Duck?"

He disappeared again into the undergrowth.

I realised my error. I just hoped it wasn't my last.

The baggage carrier also realised the gravity of the current situation and jumped off my back to scuttle around, collecting bags before donning a bullet proof vest and lurching off into the jungle with a cry of "Follow me, Bwana, if you don't wanna be duck food" but I stayed put. I would like to tell you it was through choice but it was mostly due to my foot being caught in a tree root. Anyway, we had come here together to sort a world threatening problem and we could only do that together, as a team, as two against the world or at least against the ducks; petty bickering could not be allowed to cloud the issue. Logic may be at a premium in this heat and under this much pressure and matters may have got the better of Duck but I knew that he was a logical, sensible human being...

The bullet whizzed past my left ear. Okay, so he may not be logical or sensible but, luckily, he was a poor shot and only a trainee homicidal madman.

Hey, so the world was in danger. Who cares? Surely one man can save the world, why does it need two? It wouldn't make much difference if I just shuffled under this undergrowth and laid low until Duck had gone and, hey, I'm sure he
would solve the problem all by himself without little old me. At least an alive little old me.

I lay as low as possible as you can with a large rucksack on your back and didn't make a noise. Well, apart from a small occasional whimper. It was imperative not to attract Duck's attention. I had no reason to believe that he really wanted to kill me, though that shot was a bit of a hint as was the cry of "If I ever find you, you lardy, pink faced baboon of a human being I'll pull your stupid fat head off, shoot it to bits and roast it on the next camp fire I make". Not a real threat that, you have to think, more bravado.

I lay still right up until the moment he stood on my hand. Then I let out a scream, jumped up and ran into the jungle as fast as my legs could take me.

I could hear Duck shouting, as I ran, "Come back you coward, let me shoot you and put both of us out of our miseries!" but, on reflection, thought it best to keep running. Until the pit came and met me. When I decided to fall into it. With a resounding crash.

The jungle went quiet. There was just the occasional call of the kookaburra bird, obviously lost, and the far off chiming of an ice-cream van. Luckily, I could hear no Duck.

Then "Crack!".

And again, "Crack!".

And again "Crack!!"

"Who keeps saying crack?" asked a voice to my left.

"Crack!" said the voice.

"Stop it, it's most annoying."

"Crack, crack and more crack!"

I realized I was surrounded by someone doing twig cracking impersonations.

"Where are you?" asked Duck in a friendly tone. "Because I'm coming to get you."

The voice took on a more frightening meaning now it pretended to be so friendly, like a child with a small machine gun. Or a man named Duck with a small pistol.

I felt alone, defenceless and open to death. Duck was no longer an ally. In a world threatened by the swift, cunning brutality of ducks, I was now the only one sane enough to save us and Duck was another threat to my life. I was worried and my hand stung a little. Plus, Duck had a loaded gun and had run out of crisps. I was in danger.

"Yoo-hoo, where are you?" he repeated again and again, singing crazily into the dark depths of the jungle.

"Where arrgh... you?" he cried as he fell into my pit.

I didn't tell him it was my pit or that he'd landed on my sore hand.

"Hello," I nervously said.

"Aaargh-aa-aa-aaaa-aaaah!" came a cry.

But it wasn't Duck.

There was cracking of vines.

"Who the..." asked Duck, stopping short of an expletive as another body crashed into our pit.

"Hello," he said with a perfect English accent that belied the fact that he was wearing only a neatly laundered loincloth and little else. He was also carrying a torch.

"Lights my way," he said as way of explanation. "Can I be of help?"

We looked at him.

"Now, I know what you're thinking, what is the Lone Ranger doing in the jungle but, no, I'm not the Lone Ranger, who was incorrectly named as he actually had a side-kick, Tomato, I think he was called..."

"Tonto," I corrected.

"You sure that wasn't the dog in Wizard of Oz?"

"Yes, I'm sure. That was Toto."

"Okay. I'll take your word for it. But, any road up, I'm Tarzan and I've come to rescue you and take you to safety, as long as the trees don't get in the way. Is that fine by you?"

"Well, yes..." I started nervously.

"Okay, well you just need to sign this for Health and Safety purposes and I can get on with it," as he whipped out a form from his loincloth.

"You're Tarzan?" I asked.

"Yes, I know, a little star struck no doubt but don't worry, I'm quite a modest guy, no publicity and all at no charge. All funded by the Inner Jungle Council for Better Working Relationships. Ouch."

He fell into a heap.

Duck's gun smoked.

"You, what, you, look, you... you've shot Tarzan! You've killed Tarzan!" I cried.

"The Lone Ranger, he said."

"No, he said he *WASN'T* the Lone Ranger! Why you no listen!!! He could have saved us!"

"Oh."

"And the Lone Ranger wore a mask and a hat, not a loincloth. There's a huge difference. And there wasn't a horse. Or a hat. Or a gun."

Duck looked at his gun.

"Well, there was a gun. Obviously."

Strangely, Duck looked somewhat calmer now. His eyes had lost that manic panic and he was almost smiling as he looked down at his handy work.

"Sorry. I've been a bit tense. Saving the world and all. And no crisps. In fact, that's the worst bit. The world saving I can do. Even shooting some people."

"Some people? That's Tarzan. Well, was Tarzan to be strictly accurate."

Tarzan coughed a little. I jumped down and cradled his head in my hands, one of which was still quite sore.

"Tarzan, are you okay?" I asked.

"Hey," he coughed, "good shooting, man. Accurate."

"Oh, 'twas nothing," replied Duck in a strange Texan drawl and looking at his boots.

Tarzan coughed and slumped on the floor of the pit.

"I think he's dead," I said.

"Unless you're a doctor, I'd like a second opinion," Tarzan said. "I am now though... urgh."

His life slipped away in my hands.

"Just a dying wish," he muttered with his almost definitely last breath.

Duck crouched closer, realizing the gravity of what he'd done and wanting to make amends.

"Please, bury me face down. Couldn't stand the monkeys playing with my nuts after I'm dead. Yes, I'm dead this time."

And he was.

We buried him according to his last request, in the pit, nose to the ground. Good job monkeys don't ride bikes, I thought.

Duck looked at me.

"Sorry," he said, "but my somewhat strange behaviour is somewhat explained by it being the Third Equinox Of The Mallard. This is a time of year that impacts upon me somewhat more than most, bringing a dull feel to my moods and sending me into occasional psychopathic fits where I can kill people for no apparent reason. So, no need to take this personally. It could have been anyone. Indeed, it was."

"The Third Equinox Of The Mallard?" I asked. "What about the first two?"

"I'm glad you asked. The first two culminated in the almost wholesale destruction of the human race, brought about by the dark feelings of the ducks and their close feline friends, who, luckily, they fell out with, thus avoiding the total destruction of the world as we know it during the First Equinox. The Second never quite got going due to the uptake of satellite television. But, so the story goes, the Third Equinox will be the last, with wholesale destruction and no cats. And it is now."

And with this he crumpled into a heap.

I stood around. Waiting. But Duck didn't get up. He just lay and sobbed. And sobbed. And sobbed.

Then got up.

"Okay, let's get off then. Things to do. World to save."

I was dumb struck.

The jungle was fierce and threatening in the dark, the dark that now reflected the future of the world as well as us, crisp-less and without adequate trousers in this threatened world. What would become of us? How could we get out of here and save the world?

We jumped a taxi and got to the airport in under six minutes.

Another stupid bloody meeting, another wasted day. It was getting all too much for Charlene Fulmar to take. She had been appointed Marketing Manager so why didn't those stupid men let her manage?

Ah, look on the bright side, she thought as she made her way into the depths of the underground car park, it may be almost midnight, it may have been a waste of time but, hey, it's Thursday which means it's almost Friday and when I get back to my luxury apartment in my luxury car I can crack a bottle of luxury white wine open, maybe a Vouvray, maybe a Sancerre, order some food, put some porn on the television and say "Up yours!!" to those stupid, time wasting effluent called her colleagues.

Charlene had worked her way to the top the hard way and I don't just mean not taking the lift. She'd failed at University, she'd been sacked at her first job in a burger bar and she was thrown out of her role as a waitress. But she'd read the self help books and she knew persistency is king, or queen, so she had persisted. It helped that mummy and daddy bought her an apartment, a car and a nice wardrobe of clothes and that daddy worked as Marketing Director of the company she now worked for and therefore sacked the quite capable guy who was Marketing Manager in favour of his daughter.

"You did marketing at University, didn't you?" he asked, absent mindedly one day.

"Erm no, I think it was Economics. Or was it Social History. Anyway, it was something," she added.

"Good," said her father, not listening.

It had been a baptism of fire for the first month. Well, actually, she hadn't managed to find her office for the first month but the second month was a baptism of fire. The men in the office seemed to despise her for her daddy, for her clothes and for her complete lack of understanding of what a business was, let alone how a business works.

But she'd shown them! Actually, she hadn't but, hey, she would, she'd persist, she'd show them and, if she didn't, she'd go crying to daddy and he'd help by firing all their sad asses!! At least she hoped so. It was so difficult being a woman in a man's world. Especially if you are a thick woman with no real perspective on how spoiled and ignorant you are.

As she stamped into the car park after that stupid, stupid meeting, empty and cavernous in the dark, the car park, that is, her heels clacking nosily, she was aware of something, a presence around her. This was unusual for Sheila as she was pretty thick-skinned normally.

Despite this, she didn't stop, didn't look. She knew she had to keep going. Just a hundred yards to the car now.

She could see the car shining silver in the dark of the underground car park.

But what was that on the car? A bird? A cat? Her handbag perhaps?

As she drew closer, she looked on in amazement. Was that a duck?

"Oh, funny," she thought to herself, "those men doing men things, doing silly pranks, trying to frighten me, well, it won't work, I won't be scared."

She walked confidently up to her new car.

"Hey," she started but, as she drew even closer, she heard a noise behind.

"Yes, very funny, is it Thursday?" she yelled.

There was no reply.

Then she heard a noise.

She turned, startled.

And there she saw up to fifty and maybe even sixty-seven ducks, all shuffling towards her.

She looked at them and wondered what to do. Were they dangerous? How did they get into the underground car park? Were they a present? They didn't look friendly. She had to think fast (there's a first time for everything).

So, she ran to the car.

But there the duck titled its head and seemed to smile at her.

She tripped, lost a heel and the ducks behind lifted their speed.

As she tried to raise herself they dived onto her supine body.

Her screams were not heard.

Her Sancerre went un-drunk.

And the parking would cost a lot on money once they'd found her dismembered body.

Daddy would have a vacancy.

"Hi and welcome back after the news, this is Chris Less with the morning phone in here on Here FM. Today we're talking about Burning Homosexuals: Is It Right and if so, what's the best way? This has generated a lot of callers, mostly male so far I recall, so, come on, get dialling and get involved in the debate. If you don't, I may have to make up some stuff all by myself and you wouldn't want that, would you? My producer also says no...Any way, on the line right now we have... is that Damon?"

"Yeah, mate, it's Dame here but you can call me, erm, Dame. I'm a bit nervous."

"So you should be. Well, Dame, I'm sure you have an opinion so let's put it to you: burn or spurn?"

"Well, live and let live mate, I say, but, you know, if they have to be gay, and I don't think anyone's making them be that way, if they have to be gay, I say, well, I say, if they have to be gay, burn 'em but in a humane way, not nasty like, just gently. You know, live and let live, that's what I say."

"I know what you're saying but, Dame, and I know you're nervous and probably thick but may I ask you, why?"

"Why? Blimey. I didn't realise you'd get philosophical with me. I just thought you'd say yes and offer me money. I don't think I'm actually equipped to give any resonance to my mere reasoning here, after all, I am phoning in to a poor radio show using my own money to forward what masquerades as free speech but is actually just a cheap way to broadcast."

"Excellent, next on the line we have Dave from Yorkshire. Yorkshire?"

"Yeah, just thought you may be mentioning the ducks."

"Where's Yorkshire, Dave?"

"Why haven't you mentioned the ducks?"

"Ducks?"

"Yes."

"The homo ducks you mean?"

"No, the killer ducks, they are outside, they are killing. We are surrounded by ducks."

"Oh, I get it, crank call, eh, Dave? Good one, killer ducks, yes, like it. Is it April 1st? Spaghetti trees next is it, Dave?"

"NO!!! We are being killed here! By ducks!"

"Oh, yeah, ducks. Placid animals, never met anything so kind and cuddly. And quacky. And they're killing you, yeah? Caller. Dave? Dave? Looks like we've lost him..."

SEVEN

The large duck dozed quietly in the large Yorkshire cavern, safe amongst the silence of its armed hoards. Content in peaceful slumber, it dreamt of world destruction, human casualties, controlling the world and endless supplies of soggy crusts of bread. It was happy, knowing that the plan was coming together.

The hoards did not rest so easily, however, ready and eager as they were for the next command, they sat, upright and taut, waiting for the next command so they could wreak havoc on mankind by maiming and slaughtering whomever may get in their way to world domination. So far they had been swift and economic in their onslaught, eminently successful, carrying out the virtual overthrow of Britain with few casualties in their ranks. They knew it may get worse but they knew they had systematically stripped the country of all of its vital assets in a highly professional manner as the authorities turned a blind eye and denied the facts.

The Government and its supporters refused to believe that ducks could be the most threatening factor for the future of the country, constantly repeating the mantra "if we can keep inflation to single figures we'll be out of the woods" and "if the opposition could forget their duck agenda and see what we've done for the country" then the world would be a better place. No mention was made of the fact that members of the opposition were dwindling in duck-related incidents.

"It's a conspiracy-cover-up-blinkers-over-the-eyes scenario!" shouted some faceless MP.

"Do you honestly mean to say that, in the present climate, the opposition would have us ignore the growing problems of money supply in favour of slaughtering a few ducks?" asked the Chancellor of the Exchequer in the Commons.

"Yes, you big fat pillock," came the reply from the opposition benches, "better alive and poor than dead and rich. Especially if you're going to get it from a duck."

There was uproar. Papers were waved and voices raised.

"Pillock!"

"Tit!"

"Armpit!"

"Chevalier!!"

"Pig-dog!"

"Wastrel!!!"

"Numpty!" came the cries.

"Order!" shouted the guy with a wig but to no avail.

The opposition was defeated in the vote and the Duck Bill was thrown out without even a second hearing. This would have amused the large duck who slept on as the younger ducks, who were being trained in unarmed combat, terrorist activity and how to hideously deface a human being, continued their training. And the Commons waved their papers, as ignorant of their fate as always.

In the Yorkshire cavern, there was a terrifying sound of quacking and hissing as the trainee ducks vented their wrath on the store room dummies stolen from Percy's Gents Outfitters the day before whilst, across the water, the bedraggled, torn, deflated pieces of plastic floated around, swirling in the water, a testimony to the effectiveness of the training. The trainee ducks could not wait for their time to come and their time was coming.

The large bill of the snoozing duck nuzzled into its down. One large, lazy eye opened a little to gaze at the digital watch which blazed its light from below its wing. Slowly, its head rose and from the bill came a long, controlled yet thunderous and grotesque quack.

The hoards, nervous and impatient for the signal, moved agitatedly about, heading for the plasma television at the end of the cavern.

"This is the Six O'clock News with me, Bing Bang Lardell and a woman, who is standing up for no apparent reason..." it boomed from the rather effective surround sound stereo system, "... from the BBC."

The large duck quacked quietly and contentedly under its mound of down and fat as it saw the pictures on the screen. The plan was working.

The auditorium was full and the audience expectant. Despite the strange set (white light, pink settees and a spiral staircase) they had come to see the cutting edge stand-up with the large shoes. As he appeared on stage with his strange stooping style, the audience as one burst into applause.

He looked at his large shoes and began his routine in his unique, slow, meandering yet confident style. But tonight, the audience were aghast.

"What?" he asked slowly as he heard gasps at his opening, "is it too early, too close, too shocking to talk about... *ducks*?"

His rhetorical question was met with boos and cat-calls plus a few empty crisp packets. He looked at the crowd and was about to shout "Yes, they are killers, audience, but they are just animals, we can win this, so raise your game!" but realised that he was suddenly on very shaky ground. So, ditch the Tom O'Connor material too. "Jokes have to be real, Leeds, you have to be real!"

Too late as a tomato hit him full on the forehead.

"A tomato? That's *SO* last Century, Leeds!" he yelled.

Then the auditorium went dark. There were screams and the muffled sound of down. This was one punch-line that wasn't expected. At least that tomato had saved *his* life.

The plane lifted off on time. The pilot apologized for this and to all of the people who were still on the ground because they turned up on time, and explained that this was unusual but the plane's engine had fallen off in Tunisia that very morning and, but for the fact that he hadn't been to bed due to a heavy drinking session with a Scottish gynecologist who was celebrating being drunk for twenty-two consecutive days, he may never have taken off at all.

This would have worried the passengers, had they have been listening or even on the flight.

"Still, here we are, one step nearer certain death and who really cares 'cos I don't," he continued.

Duck, like the rest of the passengers, heard none of this. He sat quiet and disconsolate next to me.

"Gosh, my head really hurts," added the pilot.

Duck brooded, one hand on his ear, looking dolefully out of the small window, noticing the stormy sky all around us. Occasionally, I tried to brighten Duck up by recounting amusing anecdotes from the rather crispy in-flight magazine but all he wanted to do was chew on one of his last, stale crisps and spill his coffee on me. It was an agonizing silence for me, broken only now and then by a scream as the coffee seeped into my underpants.

Suddenly, unexpectedly, he broke the silence.

"Get me a bourbon!" he growled as the stewardess passed, "and he'll pay" as he pointed at me.

She obliged and he gulped it down in one. His broody eye stared out at the gathering storm.

"Now, listen up everyone," the pilot's voice said, crackling over the intercom, "don't be concerned about the slight bit of turbulence, just hold your drink in two hands like I do, hahahahahahaha! Just a joke. Just make sure your glass is empty. I do. Anyway, here's a joke to help you keep your spirits up before we all plunge to our inevitable doom. There's a scuba diver and a Jehovah's witness and they go into this pub and...."

The joke faded as the intercom crackled into silence.

Duck said nothing, just sat, motionless, immune to the manic shaking of the plane and there he stayed without a word for a full twenty five minutes.

Then he spoke again.

"Where's the toilet?"

I breathed a sigh of relief as he pushed past me and made towards the toilet, not only because of the lightening of the tension but also because I was fed up of trying to dodge his coffee. My relief did not last long. The body of a smelly, grey suited man plonked itself next to me. I held my breath as he stunk to the high heavens.

"Hey, you, man, like," he started, "you been to Africa like was it? It's great, ain't it? Cool, I mean and not cool as in not hot! Hey. Look at them clouds. Just heavy. Man, really heavy. I think I'm going to be sick."

As he leaned into me I was almost overcome by the heavy smell of liquorice.

"The clouds, they're like a warning man, a warning, a message, like SMOKING CAN DAMAGE YOUR HEALTH or DON'T SWIM HERE or something like that. We're going to die. We've had it. I can just tell. It's the Equinox. The Equinox. I know."

I was hardly able to listen to him as I was trying so hard not to breathe.

But he knew. How did he know?

What did he know?

Were we all doomed?

And why is this chapter so short?

Len Horridge

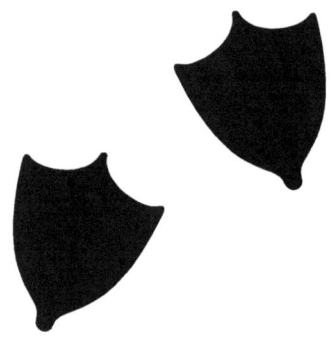

EIGHT

In the large park, the wind swept around the brown leaves, pushing and pulling them into the cold night air. A young couple, oblivious to the unusually cold weather, walked hand-in-hand in the failing light, desperately trying to stare into each others' eyes in the gathering gloom.

Saying nothing to each other, their body language speaking more volumes than mere words, they carelessly strode on down the grassy bank towards the lake. As they reached the bank, they stopped and exchanged a swift kiss, their legs brushing the longer grass that grew up from the edge of the lake. Unaware of the danger, they smiled and walked on along the curve of the bank.

Behind one of the moored rowing boats, that only months before had been this very couples' love boat, sat a fat mallard, its beak still dripping blood from a recent kill. As it heard the humans approach, it held its breath, smelling the air for the approaching smell of human flesh.

It quivered with excitement as its prey came into sight. Biding its time, it waited until the couple stopped. As they began to share meaningful glances, the mallard pounced. The air was a flurry of reeds and water.

At that moment, the young man decided that the time was ripe, this time, to tell his beloved, in the well worn ways of old, of his innermost desires and, as he was old fashioned, it was time to propose marriage. As he bent down onto one knee, the mallard flapped noisily over his head, flushing past him and careering into the might oak just over his shoulder. With an almighty quack, the mallard hit the trunk, breaking its neck on impact and sliding down the tree, dead to all the world.

"What's up?" asked the girl, oblivious to the carnage under the tree.

"Erm, nothing," replied her beloved, scratching his head in bewilderment at the crash behind him. "Nothing. Just doing my lace up, that's all."

A strange sense of déjà vu crept over him.

He'd got away lightly, on two counts. Twice.

We stumbled through customs, two tired and dispirited human beings, though none of the customs officials noticed.

I watched the fire engines flock around our grounded plane with no great compassion or care. Even the sight of the frustrated fireman kicking the plane as it refused to set alight and he therefore couldn't use his hose, was not enough to rouse my passions.

We cursed our luck. All we had to show for our journey was two full brown paper bags, an almost empty packet of crisps, a new set of crocodile luggage and an unused disposable camera. Oh and three bottles of gin.

"Here, sonny, not so quick," came a voice from behind. "Just what do we have in that little brown bag?"

It was a large, naval looking customs official who moved slowly away from his desk.

"Nothing of note," mumbled Duck.

"Let me be the judge of that, sonny," came the reply. "Now, what is in that bag?"

"You'll be sorry you asked," said Duck.

"Perhaps, sonny, but I'd like to have a look."

Duck took the bag from my grasp and gave it to the official who opened it up and looked briskly into it.

His face contorted slowly and he looked at Duck, into the bag and back at Duck.

"Bleauch," he said as he turned white the green and then fainted, his large uniformed body falling backwards to the floor. We found ourselves surrounded by uniformed officials, some with guns.

"What have you done to Mr. Archway?" they asked.

"Merely complied with his request," Duck responded.

"Which was?"

"To look into this bag."

"Right, well, I'd better have a look for myself," said the next official, grasping the bag and peering in.

There was a silence. A long silence.

Duck smiled.

The face of the large uniformed official turned white and then green, he snapped the bag shut and motioned Duck to carry on, holding his breath as he did.

"Does this mean I'm clear then?" asked Duck. "Only I thought it must, as you turned green and this is the green channel?"

Duck chuckled to himself as the official suddenly ran towards the gentleman's room, followed by his astonished colleagues. As we swept into the main arrival lounge to mingle with the masses of arrivals, Duck was still chuckling to himself. His humour did not last for long.

"Look!" he said, yelling in a way that had worried me in the past and still worried me in the future.

He ran into the crowd and pointed excitedly towards the taxi ranks, knocking over a little old lady as he did so.

She had just returned from visiting her son Derek in Australia and was none too pleased at being knocked over.

"I've come all the way from visiting my son in Australia and you knock me over on the last leg of the trip!" she cried. "How thoroughly disappointing!"

"Sorry," Duck apologized.

"Sod off you spotty faced one eyed wombat," came the reply. "That's an Australian insult for you, by the way."

Duck decided to ignore her, though he did glance back at her a couple of times with his eye on his gun. He kept running towards the taxi rank where he now fixed his gaze on a small knot of people queuing, it seemed, for a taxi.

I kept up with him as best as I could, carrying his luggage and all.

"Why the crowd?" I asked as I caught up with Duck.

"Can't you see?" replied Duck.

"Oh, yes, sorry, it's a taxi queue."

"No, you fool..." started Duck.

"Piss-pot canary sucker is better!" shouted the little old lady. "Yes, I like that one."

".. can't you see?"

I couldn't.

Duck pushed his way to the front of the queue to much abuse, luckily most of it verbal.

Duck stopped and a huge smile beamed across his face.

"At last. The saviour."

"The what?"

Two Americans took photos and, seeing this, a group of Japanese asked if they could take theirs. Nobody knew why but you couldn't miss a photo opportunity.

And, as the crowd parted, I saw a white robed figure at the front of the queue. He was short but had a transcendental aura about him which I put down to having spent 24 hours on a long-haul flight but the small crowd who had gathered looked on in awe. They gasped as he occasionally clutched at the air or now and again scratched his left ear. He was quietness personified, calm and serenity all in one person in a slightly soiled white robe until he suddenly let out the piercing scream which sounded like the sound of a wounded elk or a small person in a very bad dentist's chair.

The crowd gasped. Then there was silence.

Then he spoke.

"Yes. Yes. Wrexham have... equalised!!!"

There was a small sigh of disappointment.

It was at this moment that I noticed a small wire stretching from the inside of his robe to his right ear and I realized that the supposed trance-like state was, in fact, brought about by listening to this afternoon's football commentary on a short wave radio he had secreted about his person.

"Wrecks Ham?" asked an American from his loud shirt. "Have we been there?"

His wife studied a guide to The United Kingdom.

"Erm, no."

"Come on then let's go!" he cried and grabbed her by her arm, whisking her away.

There was an American-Japanese stampede for the taxis and, in no time, none were left, leaving the three of us alone.

Duck, his eye quivering and with a voice full of emotion spoke slowly. "This man is a man of great wisdom and understanding," he said to me in hushed tones.

"But he supports Wrexham!" I argued.

In Duck's eye there was a rekindled flame of hope and determination, a look that said "Hello, good evening and welcome" and "Watch out you ducks, we're back and we're coming to get you". Of course it may also have been saying "Sorry, we're not in, leave your message after the long quack".

Whatever, he was entranced by the man in front of us and the frustration of our trip had melted away like a pat of butter on a hot summer's day and even I started to feel a renewed optimism, or would do once I'd changed my socks. Duck looked at me as if to say "All is now not lost" though it may have been "You need some fresh socks, you know".

Though, I have to admit, I was slightly in awe of this man ... after all, he had a passion for Wrexham and that wasn't to be sniffed at. Unlike my socks.

Into the office of the Prime Minister came one of his main support staff and key confidants and advisers, Al Orange.

"Al," said the PM, "tell me, this duck thing, is it serious?"

Al laughed, nervously and had no eye contact.

"No, no, Prime Minister, the duck problem is not a problem at all, not a problem at all."

The Prime Minister eyed him suspiciously.

"You know, when you repeat yourself, Al, you always make it sound like you don't believe what you're saying."

"Is that right? Is that right? Well, no, Prime Minister, we have nothing to worry about, nothing to worry about, it's all under control, all under control."

"And you can stop that hypnotism trick, it's not working."

"It did last time," mumbled Al.

"What?"

"Nothing. Nothing. Anyway, we must…"

"So, when it comes to ducks, there is no concern, is that what you are saying?" demanded the Prime Minister from behind his large Prime Minister's desk.

"Yes. Or no."

"Which one?"

"The one that isn't the worrying one. The ducks are nothing to worry about. Nothing to worry about…"

"Stop it!"

"Sorry. But, no, or yes, they are nothing to worry about. Ducks are fine. Ducks are good. Ducks are our friend. And there have only been a few incidents in the North, so it's not that important."

"But there are reports of ducks killing people. Is that true? Is that possible?"

"Possible but possibly not true. Possibly not true at all. Though possibly could be. Just a few, anyway, not enough to get worried about. Possibly."

"But the papers..."

"Oh, you know the papers, Prime Minister, out to cause concern and chaos wherever they can, blowing a story up, making it bigger than it is and then putting their own spin on it. And that should be what we're doing after all..."

"Yes, well, keep me informed if this does become any bigger. Let me know when it's a worry."

"Oh, it's not a worry yet..."

"Yet? Not a worry yet, you say?" enquired the Prime Minister with an enquiring look.

"No, no, nothing to worry about yet..."

"Stop that! And your name. Al Orange. Not as in duck à l'orange?"

Al looked at the Prime Minister and wondered if the gaff was up. But it wasn't. Not yet.

We caught the train back to Yorkshire after a day's trek from the airport. We could have got a taxi but realized we didn't have a penny between us or, for that matter, a map of London. This gave us a chance to see what impact the ducks had had on London and, to our surprise, there was little or no impact on the capital as yet. I saw this but Duck didn't. It seemed to pass him by as he looked at the "new saviour" with glazed eyes. He insisted we return back north to confront the problems head on.

"We must return back north immediately to confront the problems head on," he tautologically said.

"Yes, I think we all know that," I narrated.

"Okay, sorry, forgot you were narrating," he apologized.

I pointed at our new friend, who had just ordered seventeen bacon sandwiches from the buffet car and was arguing frenetically with the buffet manager who was demanding payment.

Our friend kept telling him that all possession was theft, except for spiritual possession, which was a completely different kettle of fish, devouring a sandwich as he spoke. I came to his rescue but not before he told the buffet manager that his sins would be found out in "the later life", as he called it, and that Wrexham were going to be promoted this year at last and may even have a chance in the LDV Trophy.

"The day of reckoning draws ever closer for us all, oh man of the buffet car," he continued, "and paying for bacon sandwiches will be the least of your concerns. Bide you well on that thought."

"And how do you know?" asked the buffet manager.

"Well, Wrexham have drawn their last three games. It's a sign."

"A sign they can't hold onto a lead," replied the buffet manager, belying a great knowledge of lower league football.

"You may be saved," said our friend.

"Unless I'm depending on your goalkeeper," was the response.

Duck, who seemed to be capable of silent communication with our new friend, nodded to him, an act that placated the robed one, so we all moved quietly along to First Class and shuffled into our seats. It was no surprise to me that, although once again I was footing the bill, I didn't know our new friend's name. Indeed, I wasn't sure that Duck knew it despite his knowledge of the stranger's abilities.

If you looked at it realistically, I had forked out a great deal of money on one and now two people I knew precious little about. Or, to put it another way, I was a mug. But I was a mug who believed that these two people could save the world. So, I was a double mug. And I had to pay for seventeen bacon sandwiches somehow.

We sat in silence, save for the munching of the bacon sandwiches and the occasional burp.

Then both of my traveling companions started to talk in hushed tones. They talked and talked and then looked at me.

I waited for the news, maybe of salvation, maybe of world shattering news.

"What's he say?" I asked.

"Oh, I was just telling him that you'd pay for the bacon sandwiches."

Great. World destruction on the way and I'll be penniless.

They spoke again. I could hear the word "Equinox" and "Ducks" and little else. Oh, "Yes, he normally pays" was also in there. The train clattered on through the dark night but, luckily, not through any tunnels with sexual undertones.

"Stop!" our new friend suddenly said to Duck.

My thoughts ran to how much the fine was for pulling the emergency cord.

"Stop! Voices, I hear voices!"

Duck was silent, so it wasn't his voice.

"Solitary, quiet voices, it is clear, it is now clear. I know, I know now. It says..."

There was a pregnant pause as we waited anxiously to hear of our fate.

"It says, it says... we are now approaching Peterborough, please take all of your belongings with you. Change here for Cambridge. Mind the gap."

And then the intercom woman said "We are now approaching Peterborough, please take all of your belongings with you. Change here for Cambridge. Mind the gap" so he was right about that.

And with that he collapsed in a heap, either tired out by the voices or a little pogged by the seventeen sandwiches he'd just eaten without once ever going to the toilet. We were so impressed with the exactness of his prediction that we let him sleep all the way to Leeds where we were to alight and get off.

The journey was spent playing Travel Scrabble which would normally have been relaxing but Duck could only spell the names of ducks and the rather worrying "apocalypse" which was a high scorer.

We forgot about our worries until we alighted and got off at Leeds where, in the misty surroundings of platform six, reality reared its ugly head again.

"Eter Ugh Aised U Thugh Gound!" called the newspaper vendor.

"Pardon?" we asked.

"Eter Ugh Aised U Thugh Gound!" called the newspaper vendor again.

"Eh?"

"I said Eter Ugh Aised U Thugh Gound!" repeated the newspaper vendor.

And then I looked at the headline to the paper he was holding. Indeed the newspaper vendor was right as the headline read "Eter Ugh Aised U Thugh Gound!".

Blimey, I thought, just an hour or so ago we were there and now, just minutes after we left, Peterborough had been raised to the ground. The ducks had just missed us but it seemed that they were onto us. Maybe they realized the threat, maybe it was just chance, maybe it's because I'm a Londoner that I love London town.

Whichever way, there was trouble. We needed to get back home and, like a constipated mathematician, work it all out. But not with logs.

"But look," interrupted our new friend. "A small crumb of comfort?"

He pointed to the stop press.

There, nestling in among the stories of horror attacks on people, the inability of the police and armed forces to stem the duck attacks, the listing of the names of the dead, there was the news that our new friend was looking for, a beacon of light in this darkest of days.

"Stop press…" I read. "Full time scores. Colchester 2, Wrexham, 1".

Our new friend let out a groan. We knew that we were entering the long dark evening of the night before the day after. May we all be saved.

The small duck walked along the deserted Yorkshire street. Empty plastic bottles blew around, oblivious to their current role in the narrative. The duck sniffed the air and, sensing human activity, its devil senses kicked into gear, and it closed in on the potential targets.

It had been well trained.

Most of these devil ducks had been trained to hunt in pairs or larger groups, thus necessitating the need to use the collective noun, but this one had been trained as an individual. It had been given orders to just "go out and cause a bit of mayhem" (though, actually, in duck language, this was merely a load of high pitched quacking and a point of a wing in a vague yet general direction).

So, it had set off and had soon found a small, almost un-spoilt village (save for the rather large houses on the hill which kind of said "Hey, look at the money we've got, triple garages and all, and you peasants down the hill can only just afford the price of a pint! Though, obviously, our presence will have had an impact on your house prices so why not sell up and realize the huge equity jump you've experienced because of us?"), set in the middle of large, animal filled fields.

As the duck stood in the main street, it could see a church, a post office a shop and a solitary pub. The church clock showed it was just before four o'clock so the duck knew where to find its prey. It sniffed the air and knew it was right.

The pub was the focal point of the village. Built almost one hundred years ago, it had steadfastly refused to become one of the "new breed" of pubs that had so blighted the landscape. It was a traditional pub and a traditional pub it would stay.

Catering for drinkers and the occasional hiker, this was a village community pub and was proud of it. Here you would find hand-pulled bitter, mild and normally a very strong guest ale. This week it was Big Dangly Donkey, 8.5% proof, only two pints per person, please, no naked flames, and it was proving a popular pull.

Three regulars sat at the bar. Drinking. Talking. Reading. Thinking. Drinking.

Elsewhere in the unsuspecting pub, five or six other people talked and drank in the misty, smoke filled air. It was late afternoon but the drinking continued. It was not a jolly but neither was it a somber atmosphere in there. It was just drinking, as usual. The talk was occasionally of ducks but the resident drinkers played this down. Death, of course, would eventually come to them all but death would never come to their village in the shape of a duck.

Then the door blew open, the chattering stopped and the CD player continued to play "Don't Stop Me Now" by Queen.

And there, in the open door, stood a duck.

The regular drinkers stopped quaffing their bitter and mild and looked up.

There was no panic.

"Have you heard about these ducks?" asked Sam.

"Yes, that's one, there, at the door. They're killers, so they say," said Steve, sarcastically.

"Well, they think they're hard, do they?" asked Sam.

"Well," replied Steve, "so they think."

Debbie, the landlady, eyed the duck.

"Oi, you, duck!" she called to the duck at the door, "yes, you, you little duck, you get out! You're barred."

And the duck, knowing when it was onto a bad thing, closed the door quietly and slipped away into the afternoon, leaving the regulars at The Fox to continue their drinking in peace.... until, just a few minutes later, the door blew open again and the ghost of William Shakespeare appeared, slightly shimmering, at the door.

"And you're Bard, too!" shouted the regulars in unison.

NINE

The Reverend Albert Sprocket picked his nose and stood alone in the pulpit of his empty church, The Church of Saints Arnold, James and Bridget. Correctly garbed, ready for his Sunday sermon, he impatiently awaited the arrival of his normally sparse congregation, tapping his foot to the tune of "For Those In Peril On The Sea" on the wood of his pulpit.

Things had not being going terribly well for Albert of late. His congregation had been dwindling gradually away to almost nothing and he had not been aided by his sudden and rather over-zealous campaign to damn all people who used paper handkerchiefs. Some of his congregation had found his outbursts about this somewhat distancing not to say alienating. The infamous sermon just a fortnight ago Sunday in which he told all that anyone who had ever worn the colour purple, either on their body or on a close friends', or those who had kept hamsters (even if just for a weekend as a favour for a relative) or those who liked mountain bikes, would all be doomed to burn in the fiery furnaces of the devil's gardens, had not actually been seen as a positive by the small congregation and he had understandably seen the following weeks' numbers being limited to the terminally deaf or those who stumbled into the Church hoping there was a jumble sale on.

It wasn't that Albert didn't like hamsters, purple or mountain bikes or, for that matter, paper handkerchiefs, it was just that he was pretty bored doing what he was doing and there was also the small matter of the spiritual visitation that told him that the world was now doomed so he may as well have a bit of fun with those suckers who thought that religion was a water tight concept instead of a mystical concept for the gullible and homeless. So Arthur decided to come clean. And that didn't go down well.

The visitation, by the way, may have been real or not.

It may have had something to do with his home brewing kit, which should have been returned after a product recall by the manufacturers. Or the other stuff he was now using, thinking it was actually sherbet.

Whichever way, Albert now had a new mission in life: to prepare everyone for the blazing pits of Hell, and that included himself.

It's natural for people to shy away from such views, especially since Albert resembled a rather old and ugly donkey, so instead of putting on their best hats and suits this Sunday, most people had decided to shun the church and stay in bed on Sundays from now on. This saved all that dressing up malarkey and meant you could drink even more on Saturday. After all, if you do go to the trouble of getting up early and putting on your Sunday best, you want a couple of songs, a quiet prayer, an uplifting reading and a sermon that lets you go back home to cut the grass in peace. "You're all saved, enjoy your Sunday roast", that sort of thing. Such platitudes were not in Albert's vocabulary at present.

"Your ankles will hurt, your knees will burn and your brain will be screwed into your eyes so tight that blood will seep out of your ears." That was one of his latest.

Most people in the congregation had been mostly bemused by the sudden change in Albert's demeanor and behaviour; up until a fortnight ago he had been mostly mild mannered to the point of tedium and he had never said boo to the proverbial goose, but, then again, he'd never come across a goose he had felt like saying boo to anyway. Yet now, the congregation's Sunday morning snooze as they were "saved" to the sounds of a gentle yet subtly off key choir had been shattered as the Reverend had decided to turn into a frantic raving cleric who constantly shouted "Fires, you are doomed to the fires!!" and pointed out that reading the Bible wasn't going to save you.

"May as well read the Yellow Pages," was a line he was quite proud of.

"And I know this now as The Lord himself visited me whilst having a bath. That's me having a bath, of course, not The Lord. He doesn't need baths, well, not as many as the rest of us. Anyway," he carried on to the bemusement of the small gathering," he told me two things. One, watch out for that home brew as it really did have a product recall and when any home made wine puts holes in bottles you know it needs something adding to it and, two, due to a shortage of space in Heaven, He was beginning to rationalize a bit, so nobody's coming 'up here' for the next couple of million year at the earliest. He's doing an extension and it will take time. It's difficult finding builders up there, you know. 'Anyway, you probably want to know why', said the Lord."

The Lord waited for a reply.

"Oh, yes, I do, sorry Lord."

"That's okay and don't do that with the loofah. You'll be damned. Oh, sorry, you will be anyway, so carry on. Anyway, too many people have latched onto this redemption lark and I had to let them in. Frustrating but, you know, I made the rules so I had to stick to them and after a while it got a little cramped up here. Between you and me, most should be down you-know-where but, hey, what are you going to do? Well, being The Lord, there was something I could do and I've done it. Nobody up here for a while. Don't wait for the call, Arthur. Okay?"

"That's Albert, actually."

"Whatever."

Before Albert could say anything, The Lord checked off his name from his holy clipboard and disappeared. He then quickly reappeared and enigmatically added "Oh, and watch out for Ducks. With a capital D."

The Reverend Albert Sprocket was too numb to take in the last comment and sat in the bath for two hours trying to take in the news about his lack of salvation. He was awoken from his thoughts by his housekeeper, Mrs. Armitage, whom he told of his visitation as she looked enviously at his loofah. This was the last time he ever saw her. And his loofah.

He decided that he had to tell his congregation the news as soon as possible and he was going to assure them that the visit was probably a mistake but, hey, why take any chances? But when he started to tell the startling news to the few loyal members of his congregation, he had seen such hysteria and fear that he actually started to enjoy the power he didn't realise he had, so laid it on thicker with each sentence. He suddenly grew into a terrifying orator, so terrifying that the entire congregation of seven had decided not to bother coming anymore.

It was now approaching one o'clock and even Albert, in his current demented state, was beginning to realise that nobody was going to come. A dead waste of the sermon he had written which included the lines "burns so hot that eyebrows will fall off" and "like a giant slug eating your insides with a blunt fork". Or was it? If nobody would come then Albert would go out onto the streets and take his message to the world! He edged down from the pulpit, down the aisle and out of the church into the glowing afternoon sun. The streets, he noticed, were deserted, the air quiet and still.

He walked and walked for miles and did not see a soul, let alone one to save or at least damn, in Albert's case. As his mind went over the religious ranting of his proposed sermon, he was blissfully unaware of the shape which stalked him from the rooftops above.

Suddenly, Albert stopped and laughed out loud.

"Why? Why did The Lord visit me in the bath?"

From the roof above, the duck looked at its target and swooped down.

"And what was that about Ducks? With a capital D?"

His end was speedy yet bloody. He screamed but Albert's scream went largely unnoticed. He fell to the ground in a bloody, quivering heap as the bill of the duck pierced his head and split it in two. Albert lay silent and quite dead.

From the bowels of the earth came a low satisfied cackle.

And Arthur, sorry, Albert did not wake up in Heaven.

We caught a taxi at the station.

"We will go to my house!" announced Duck, suddenly.

I was a bit naffed off as I had no idea where Duck lived.

"Where's that?" I asked.

"Oh, in Otley, just a stone's throw away from Knaresborough, really, for those who are not familiar with the topography of the area we are now in," expostioned Duck.

I pointed out that I was the narrator here and therefore responsible for any plot clarification but he pointed out that he still had a revolver so I shut up and got into the taxi, not mentioning Otley's proximity to Knaresborough.

We made our way to Duck's country hide-away, which to be technically correct was just outside of Otley. Not really that close to Knaresborough at all at least not as close as Harrogate.

I had no idea that Duck was from Otley but I knew precious little about the man at all; I was similarly ignorant about our white robed friend, yet here I was, in the midst of the greatest threat the world had ever known, sitting in the back of a taxi with them, not knowing either. I just have this trusting nature. I trusted Duck when he said that we should relax in an effort to concentrate our minds for the task ahead.

I also trusted him when he whispered to me that he was expecting our young messiah to give a divine suggestion on how to alleviate the threat of the ducks, something I had serious reservations about since all he could say at present was "Colchester, how could we lose to Colchester? I can't get my head around this!" I needed him to get his head around the ducks otherwise, somewhat like Wrexham, we would all be defeated.

Our taxi driver was more loquacious, using a very bad cockney accent, somewhat incongruously given we were in Yorkshire.

"Well, guv'nor, cor blimey, where would you like to go me old cock sparrer?"

We informed him of our destination.

"Otley, squire, Otley? You jokin' me? Otley? Blimey, as if I'd know where Otley was!" And then his accent suddenly changed. "Actually, I do, only joking you, as the actress said to the giraffe when it came into the bar with a long face."

"That's a horse with a long face, I think you'll find," I corrected.

"Oooh, get you, squire, quite the funny one, ain't we? Ain't that a zebra?"

"No, it's..."

"Anyway, what you gents doing venturing out on a cold dark night like tonight all by yourselves?" he asked, keeping the cockney accent going.

"There are three of us," I pointed out.

"That's easy for you to say, squire, but you know what it's like today. Nobody's safe."

We didn't respond. We were too busy wondering why he'd just jumped his second red light and what the smell was, though we had a fair idea about the smell.

"You must be free brave men."

"Free?"

"Yeah, free of you. One, two, free."

"Free? How do you spell free?"

"You don't spell free, squire, it's a number."

"Do you say Smiff as well?"

"Not as I fink, mate."

I decided to let him concentrate but he kept up his verbal barrage of cockney nonsense, telling us of life on the road, who he'd had in the back of his cab, the percentage of people who had died of heart attacks or pure boredom whilst he'd been driving them, how many people he'd knocked down that week and his best score at ten pin bowling.

"Twenty? Is that all?"

"Yes, had a lucky day."

Apparently he'd killed more people at the wheel than he'd ever scored at ten pin bowling.

"But never got a point on my license."

"How's that?" I asked, incredulously.

"Easy, found a loophole. Haven't got a license."

I decided that, after that, I would say little to him apart from the odd "Watch out!" the occasional "People!" the regular "We drive on the right here" and "No!!" and the optimistic "Are we there yet?", which we weren't.

As we hit our fourth or fifth cyclist, I stopped counting and started praying. Ironically, the ducks may have been less of a personal threat to us than this dolt.

"As I said to her, me old Dutch that is, listen up, my old China, me old cock sparrer, the problem with the world today is the footballers and the foreigners, who don't talk our language and, of course, the government and film directors, I mean, we haven't got over the loss of Stanley Kubrick with his distant and often de-humanising view of the world which often reflects the nihilism of my own world view, though faced with seven strippers and a duck my view may be somewhat different, if you get my drift, squire…"

I wasn't paying attention but then did.

"Did you say duck?"

"Where?" screamed the driver and swerved around the road, forcing other cars into lampposts and oncoming traffic before executing a perfect three point emergency stop.

The taxi shuddered to a shuddering halt… and a rumpled cyclist fell off the roof.

The cabbie turned to me, eyes bulging, face ashen, to see us all in an undignified lump in the back of his taxi. "Where's the duck, then?" he asked.

"Erm", I began, embarrassingly from under the other two, "I thought I heard you say something about a duck. Did you mention a duck at all?"

"Me? Mention a duck? You are surmising that I actually listen to the rubbish what comes from my own gob? Blimey, I stopped listening to myself years ago. I'd be madder than my old Dutch now if I listened to half the garbage what I come out with."

"But you did mention a duck?"

"Well, be that as it may, I may have, I may not have but you going mentioning it, well, I fought my number was up, what with what is going on with the current duck situation. I mean, I'm not a coward or one of those conscientious objectors or the like but those feathered things put the willies up me so they do and right. Terrorising innocent citizens, killing stuff and what do the government do? Nothing! You can't walk safely around the streets today, what with ducks around, blimey, guv'nor, they're more dangerous than my driving, honest to goodness they is. The city ain't safe and I remember the blitz..."

"The city, you say?" I asked.

"Yes, can't get in there now, the only safe place is the country."

"Hang on. How old are you?"

"Firty free."

"You can't remember the blitz. You're too young."

"That's easy for you to say. It left its scars."

I decided not to argue.

"London's had it, my old home town," he continued, apropos of nothing, a tear in his eye.

"London. Not Leeds, then?"

"Nah, not Leeds, London, razed to the very ground this very afternoon, shortly before they got Peterborough. Ear, why you no know that, you been up the jungle or summit?"

Len Horridge

"Well, actually, pretty much so, so if you can tell us what's happened it would help me and the exposition of the story which, to be fair, has been hazy at the best of times."

And he did, once he'd got us on our seats and made sure that our seat belts where firmly buckled "not that they'd save you if I crashed" he laughed "but it means you're a captive audience, ha-ha!" and this captive audience really were captivated by what he was to tell us, well, it took our minds off his driving.

"Where shall I begin?" he asked, rhetorically, as cabbies often, nay, always do.

He told us, in his shambling faux-cockney way, how The Ducks had finally started on London just hours before and laid waste the capital city in no time, attacking the Houses of Parliament, Buckingham Palace and other major landmarks but keeping clear of The City as "well, you know the types they have there". They then carried on up the country stopping only at Peterborough, being called further north, maybe attracted to a central point in the north of the country where perhaps their leader lived, as if a quiet signal had been sent to the marauding masses. Their wok done in the south, they had now left the blighted cities they had laid waste so speedily, so frighteningly.

"We watched from the hills as cities burned slowly down to the foundations, and, as the lost citizens came from the destruction below, they joined us in a silent vigil, all of us realizing that we were watching the death of a nation, killed and overcome by those cute little things we'd been feeding our tit-bits to each weekend. From the distance of the hills we saw explosions, saw buildings collapse, heard the screams of the countless victims. We were hopeless and helpless in the eye of the onslaught, we could do nothing but sit and watch in silence at the destruction of this once great country at the hands of, or at least the wings of, these devil ducks. We were one huge mass of lost souls witnessing the death of a country. As silence engulfed us, we realised we were human, we were British and we had to do something. Some last effort, some defiance, a sign that we would never be defeated. As one, we all broke into a hymn together as we tried to lift our dispirited souls, lost, as we knew we were, we had to cling to the only hope we had left, our faith."

We were silent as this was almost poetic, well, for a taxi driver it was.

"What hymn was it?" I asked.

"Well, since it was a mostly secular bunch of people, the only song we actually knew the words to was YMCA by The Village People, so we sang that. With all the actions, mind. It was genuinely moving in more ways than one."

We fell silent again, for different reasons this time.

He told us that the initial incidents in the north were just the tip of an iceberg. All over the country there were countless stories of killings at the hands and beaks of ducks, ignored as freak accidents at first, then taken seriously as the deaths mounted into the hundreds, thousands and then millions. The press, at first under strict instructions from the government, to keep quiet and avoid mass panic, broke ranks when a top DJ was killed closely followed by the winner of a recent reality television programme. This initial blackout only made the killings more mythical and many people started to flee the cities and then the country but many stayed before they realized it was too late: The Ducks had a grip on the country that was now going to be difficult to break, especially as the armed forces, stripped to a bare minimum over the years due to some dodgy oversees deployment, could offer little defence.

In fact, Britain was slowly being cut off from the rest of the known world and some bits that were as yet unknown. The rest of the world didn't seem too bothered by this either. The rest of the world had troubles enough without breaking sweat over a little island that once had colonial rights over most of the planet; so, it was in trouble now, big deal. They were just not going to help us out.

And who said we were xenophobic?

"They is lookin' for sumfing here", he carried on, resorting back to faux cockney, "we just don't know what it is. The mother ship or something someone said on the radio. The reason for their existence, the reason for their being, the means of their destruction."

"We are all searching for the reason for our existence," said our robed one.

"Maybe they is lookin' for that large guy called Markus."

We sat, silenced by this.

"You know, he's about seven foot two, had him in my cab once..."

"Sorry," I interjected, "a large guy called Markus?"

"Yeah, you know, very tall, huge muscles, from Helsinki, I think. Any road up, he's definitely a Finn. Maybe they is lookin' for him."

I felt he may be onto something. Maybe Markus was their quarry.

"He could be right," I suggested. "They could be after Markus from Helsinki."

"Don't be daft, it's too early for the Big Finnish," said Duck.

Duck looked at me. His look made my blood run cold. If it wasn't that then what was it? The cabbie said the mother ship. The mother ship?

Was it any coincidence that The Ducks arrived at the time I came upon Duck himself? Why, now they had paralysed the country had Duck decided it was time to come back here? The means of their destruction?

And why did we flee the country for no apparent reason? And why did the taxi driver still keep hitting cyclists and how many cyclists were now left in this county?

Oh, and why was he called Duck?

I'd never thought of that...

The large gym at the north end of the city was a popular place with oversized people with too much money who wanted to be seen to be losing an ounce or two from their flabby bodies but who were much too lazy to ever really put much effort in to get down to their fighting weight. It was a poser's paradise more than a gym and the owners knew it, fleecing the fools for as much as they could with a three month penalty for cancellation of the outrageous annual fee.

It was getting late but there were still some revelers at the gym plus some people who were actually there to run, swim, play tennis or make their pecks look large. But there weren't many left at eleven o'clock at night.

LJ, as he was known to his mates, well, to his mate as he really only had one and even that was more acquaintance than mate, flopped out of the swimming pool. It was empty. He was happy to tell anyone that he was in training for a half marathon event in which he would raise a lot of money for charity. Most would have given him money to cover up his flaccid little white skinned body with the intermittent grey hair but he was too ignorant to know this or the fact that he constantly smelled of onions, even in the shower.

His purple shorts flapped around his stick like legs as he walked to the steam room.

Opening the glass door he was hit by a flush of hot steam. He made his way in, squinting his eyes to see if anyone else was in there. Nobody else was. He sat down, alone, as usual, with his thoughts and a faint whiff of onion. His hair, grey, greasy and thinning, wafted around his ill-shapen head in a pathetic attempt to escape.

He was alone with his thoughts.

Or so he thought. He sensed a movement from the corner. He couldn't see anything but he could hear something.

"Hello?" he asked to no reply. "Hello? Is there anyone there?"

All he could hear was a slalloping sound.

"My name's LJ I'm an international consultant in Holistic Solutions," he said, carelessly.

There was no reply. "I own my own company. Strategic Holistic International Training."

Then he felt something touch his foot. Slimy. Slightly furry. But not a cat.

"Hello?" he said again as the duck tufted up against his leg and cut straight into an artery.

LJ's cries were not heard by the attendant at the pool-side. The attendant also did not see what was currently happening in the Jacuzzi.

There, the blonde woman with the tied back hair, belly button piercing and reshaped breasts was trying to get a signal on her mobile phone. She was having no luck. She needed to contact her husband to let him know about the divorce but she couldn't get a signal. She also didn't know his mobile number. But she thought she could ring his mother and let him know. But she couldn't get a signal.

She cursed quietly, put the phone at the side of the Jacuzzi and sat back to relax. After all, it had been a tiring day, shopping, lunching and visiting the solicitor to put the final touches to the divorce thing. She deserved this relaxing moment at the end of the day and she was going to enjoy it.

But what was that on her toe? Oh, no, she thought, not somebody else in the Jacuzzi? She opened her eyes and, no, nobody else. So, what was that on her toe? And her toe again? What was going on?

Under the bubbles, two little ducks, with small scuba equipment, eyed the toes, so well manicured, so perfectly re-fashioned, so clean and so ready to be bitten. Which they did.

The bite did not immediately take effect. Then it did. With a look of shock on her face, the blonde woman was pulled slowly under the water where two ducks would keep her until the breath was taken from her body and her lungs filled up with water. Just before her face sunk under the bubbles, she let out a piercing scream. But the attendant did not hear her.

Back in the changing rooms, the young man flexed his muscles and caught a glimpse of himself as he made for his locker. He was pleased at what he saw. Raw meat, a real treat. Rippling, brown, powerful and unintelligent.

He looked at the lockers. What number was it? 201? 202? 203? 322??

He looked down at his key. 87, yes, that's it.

And he walked over to 87.

His locker. He hoped.

There was nobody in the locker room, save for him. The last locker to be emptied that night.

He opened the locker and thought "I don't remember that" as the duck flew into his muscled neck and pulled the life from him. He fell to the floor with a resounding thud and the attendant heard nothing.

The attendant had been made redundant in a cost cutting exercise just the week before.

And now the gleaming steel of the night time gym reflected the fires that the ducks had started as it began to burn swiftly to the ground. There was the noise of the fire engine sirens that peeled into the night but, in this case and maybe for others, it was too late.

The gym, as the human race, would not be saved.

On our arrival just outside of Otley we paid the taxi driver £467 (credit cards accepted) which apparently included VAT and drama tax but we thanked him for the information if not his driving. On the roof, a lone cyclist moaned for us to open the door and let his foot out, which we did.

We walked up Duck's gravel path to his cottage. It was small but quite nice, actually, and not what I'd imagined, looking as pretty and welcoming as the menace outside was so cold and, erm, menacing.

Duck made us a supper of prawn and vinegar crisps, au gratin of course, with a side salad of salad, which was filling if slightly over-cooked, before settling us down for the night. He took no precautions, given the plight we were in, putting his pajamas over his jungle suit and leaving a machete down his right bed-sock. He told us to forget what we had seen and heard and settle down for a good night's rest, as the task ahead of us was a daunting one, especially as the first task of the day was to get groceries from the corner shop which may or may not still be there. I said I'd stay at home and do the washing up which eased his mind considerably. Unlike my mind when he pointed to the one bed, which he expected us all to share.

"This is essential for our security," he pointed out, "we must stick together".

"Oh, okay then," we agreed.

But this close?

As it happened, we didn't. Duck snored so loud that we took our pillows and moved to the spare room where our robed friend decided to sit up all night and chant mantras to the ceiling, therefore keeping me awake, though he did drown out the snoring, I suppose.

From where I sat, I could see right up his white robe, which was not a pretty sight, but at least his moaning, sorry, mantras, were giving me some hope. Until he started going on about Ivor Allchurch, whom I surmised was a saviour of his
religion whom he kept calling on for the salvation of the world against the threat of The Ducks. Since I wasn't going to sleep anyway, I decided to ask if this assumption was correct.

"The ducks?" he replied, eyes closed but face screwed up.

"Yes, what does Ivor know about the ducks? Do you think that he can he help us from The Ducks?"

"Ducks? Ducks is in cricket," he enigmatically replied, "now, can I get back to my trance like state?"

"Yes, but what does he say? Did he see them kill my dog? Did he see the wholesale slaughter of our citizens? Is he aware that they may look cute but, in fact, they are killers? Does he have any answers?"

I stopped nervously awaiting the reply.

"I'm not sure you're treating this with the gravity it deserves," I opined as he giggled on.

"Oh, I am, don't you know, it's just that Ivor told me the one about the Welsh Fusilier and the crocodile... okay, it's an old one but it's a cracker! Haven't heard it in years but he tells it so well. Sorry, you mentioned ducks? "

"Yes, I did!"

"Duck's what?"

"No, not Duck but ducks!"

"Oh," he said as he uncrossed his legs, forgetting that he was perched on the end of the bed and he slapped to the ground with a large bump, thus making him moan again, though this time for good reason.

"Well," he said, "I can see into the future but I didn't foresee that."

"Oh, and pull your robe up, would you, your muse is showing..."
I added.

In the dark, foreboding cavern, a small group of ducks were pouring over their list.

The waterproof paper, gained just days ago after the pillaging of a small corner shop in Pontefract, had a long list of towns, cities, villages and municipal locations. All were now in the hands, or to be technically correct, the wings, of the ducks. These were the places they had lain waste, murdering innocent people as they went, destroying buildings, smashing infrastructure and occasionally getting a free bath in a garage car wash. Their map of Britain was a map of terror and destruction.

The list was a long one.

They quacked in contentment as they looked at it.

Colchester, Solihull, Bath, Retford, Mansfield, Bracknell, Stoke-on-Trent, Exeter, Market Harborough, Uttoxeter, Bakewell, Todmorden, Bentley, Wainfleet All Saints, North Somercoats, South Somercoats, Hunmanby, West Heslerton, East Heslerton, Market Weighton, King's Lynn, Corby, Market Deeping, Melton Mowbray, Lutterworth, Fenny Compton, Temple Herdewyke, Cubbington, Bedford, Yardley, Gobion, Moreton Pinkney, Long Buckby, Nobottle, Ledbury, Banbury, Ampthill, St. Neots, Biggleswade, Wyboston, Horringer, Great Cornard and many others.

Ducks, you may have noticed, are not alphabetically minded. They are not dyslexic, not even Killer Ducks who are on the whole uneducated, it's just that they don't really give a damn about the alphabet and grammar and the like (a bit like the author). They just like killing people and making lists. They are also not very hot on geography. But they don't care.

They ignored this slight explanatory bit by the author and got back to the list in hand, or, in their case, wing.

The list was an impressive one of their conquests and the ducks patted themselves on the back at their own success. Yet, as their eyes scanned the list, they stopped and eyed each other in shock and maybe even horror.

At the bottom of the list they had to shake their collective beaks, realising that they could not conquer all.

They therefore used their devil fangs to bite off the bottom name and let it float out of the huge cavern.

Even a Killer Duck baulks at Glasgow...

I woke up and walked downstairs.

"Want some tea?" asked Duck as he took a cup in one hand and the teapot in the other.

"That sounds good," I responded, blinking the summer sunshine that was spewing forth through the window into my early morning yes.

"Heard the news?" asked Duck.

"No. What?"

Duck was making bacon and eggs as he talked. No crisps in sight.

"Well, it seems that the government got their backsides in gear, found the lair of the ducks and nuked them all last night. So, the threat from the ducks is over. Of course, there's a bit of nuclear fallout to worry about..."

"But that's brilliant," I replied, wiping the sleep from my eyes, "just brilliant. Great news!"

"Oh, well, fallout can be nasty but luckily but I actually put lead in all of the walls over night so we'll be okay, I think. That guy outside looks a little agitated, mind."

Outside, our milkman was writhing on the orange lawn, large cows coming out of his ears.

"Want some tomatoes?" asked Duck and started to juggle with his three arms.

"Oh, no, this isn't a dream sequence, is it?" I asked, knowingly.

"No, I always ride around with a small armadillo on my back, you stupid fool!" yelled Duck as he ran around the walls of my flat and I realised that it was time to wake up and leave this stupidly optimistic yet surreal dream behind.

I awoke and the ducks were still here. Though, on the bright side, there was no fallout and my lawn was still green. Well, greenish.

"And we're only two thirds of the way through," added Duck from my dream.

"But listen," said the young man in the nice suit, "it's a sign but maybe it's not a bad sign. You know, maybe this is just a way of punishing those who have done some bad in the world. Maybe the ducks are a work of god. Maybe this is god saying, hey, if you do some good, you're saved!"

"Oh, yeah, god or a god. He'd do that, right?"

"Well, yes, he would. And if you read the reports of the killings closely, all of those who have been killed so far have been, well, less than perfect people, people with faults and pasts, people who maybe just deserved to die."

"So, your god says certain people deserve to die?"

"I'm not saying that, I'm just saying, well, maybe, just maybe it's a sign?"

"A god who likes to kill. Not much of a god then? Bit nasty, I'd say. Live and let live and all that."

"Yes, but maybe it's not real, it's just a sign, an allegory, a way of making others see the error of their ways, you know, that correction is better than cure, that if...."

"And maybe it's just the author killing off certain types of people he doesn't really like and using the ducks as an excuse. Maybe he's just indulging in a very childish fantasy where he is actually showing his impotence in the world and is just relieving his own frustration through words?"

"Well, obviously, there's that as well. But that wouldn't fit into my belief based system of explaining such phenomena. Though I may put that in my essay if that's okay..."

Next morning the glistening sun pierced the dew leaden windows of Duck's cottage to wake us at an unearthly hour. None of us had slept well.

Duck prepared a breakfast of toasted prawn and vinegar crisps with milk and sultanas which was eaten with remarkable alacrity by none of us, even our alba robed chum, who limped into the kitchen holding his knee and moaning softly in another show of religious fervour, or maybe it was just in pain.

The sun sped through the window of the kitchen, past the imitation Welsh dresser and straight into Duck's smiling face, where it beamed back into our faces, blinding us. Duck was in high spirits, I was in sunglasses.

This was strange after the distressing news of yesterday and once again raised my concerns about his true role in this entire farrago. There was no disguising his glee this morning. I asked if he'd had a good dream.

"Dream, no, but a vision, well, almost a vision", he explained in which all three of us were floating along on a calm azure blue river in a golden boat as huge crowds roared their ticker-tape welcome as saviours of the world as they shouted "Our heroes", "Thanks for saving us" and "The cheque's in the post" as we sailed past.

The crowd feasted on huge portions of crispy fried duck with a side salad of salad and balsamic vinegar. He said it was a sign. I thought it was sign that he'd eaten all the wrong things and suggested he checked the sell-by-dates on the crisps.

"What do you think, Bernard?" asked Duck.

"I think it's my cartilage, maybe a groin strain, could take a couple of weeks," replied our friend in white who, it turned out, was called Bernard.

"Bernard? He's called Bernard?" I asked, choking on a sultana. "He doesn't look like a Bernard". And then I stopped; who *DOES* look like a Bernard, after all.

"What does he look like then?" asked Duck.

"My elbow has a small scrape, too."

"Erm, I thought more of a Derek?"

"I don't often dream," Duck continued, ignoring my response, "but when I do, I'm right... so maybe we should have a picnic. Once we've been to the corner shop."

I was at great pains to point out the current danger lurking outside but he was not in the mood to listen this morning, "No, my vision is true, we must go out, we must celebrate my vision, we must ensure that we are not afraid. The only thing to fear is fear itself."

"I'm terrified," I admitted but, when I looked up, Duck had gone. I grabbed Bernard and ran out into the garden but he was nowhere to be seen. In the trees the birds chirped happily, squirrels ran after their nuts and small voles kept out of sight; it was a vision of calm. But we couldn't find Duck, well, to be honest, I couldn't as

Bernard was too busy rubbing his elbow to look, Duck had just gone. The day shone golden yet I shivered, as Mother Nature, the very mother of these devil ducks, showed off her finery.

We sped along in the car shouting "Duck" out of the windows. Good job nobody was around as we'd either have been arrested or a lot of people would have been ducking.

Then I heard that dreadful noise.

"Hi, I'm here."

And there, in the back of the car, was Duck with a huge hamper for our picnic.

"How long have you been there?" I asked.

"All of the time."

The picnic held no thought of enjoyment for me, only fear, fear of the ducks, fear of death and fear that someone may recognize me with these two lunatics.

I closed my eyes and tried to think of nice things, the days before the ducks came, Christmas lights, holidays in Filey, hand pulled beer and mittens. Which was a daft thing to do as I was driving. The farmer in whose field we landed kind of
accepted this story, looking at my two colleagues as a method of explaining my eccentric behaviour.

"Oh, I'm not related!" I said, rather too quickly.

We moved onto our picnic spot quickly, by the side of a babbling river that curved slowly around its own bend and into a small group of oak tress which hid the world from us.

The sun beamed down on us and we were oblivious to ducks, though we never checked for any.

The tranquility had trapped us.

Duck opened the wine, we had a drink and we all seemed to visibly relax, removing the normally pessimistic shroud that had covered us over the last few days, how many days I didn't know as I had lost count and my diary. Bernard sat on the bonnet of the car, cross-legged, head up into the sky, contemplating and murmuring whilst quaffing his wine with his eyes closed. Luckily it was white wine as he missed his mouth quite regularly. He did not inspire my confidence but he inspired the confidence of Duck.

"Now's he's here, we will be fine," said Duck as Bernard slipped slowly off the bonnet of the car and spilled his glass of wine all over his robe. "He has powers even he doesn't understand."

"Like the ability to sit up straight?" I asked. "Doesn't seem to have mastered that one yet. Or the ability to drink."

"His powers are above ours. He does not need basic skills. And he will save us. Save us all."

"But he seems a bit... simple?"

"Ah, yes, his very naivety will be what saves us. You may not see this now but he has a simpler view of the world which we, in our sophisticated way, cannot see. His simpleness, if that's a word, gives him clarity of vision. The world is simpler than we think and Bernard is simpler still."

Okay, I wanted to say, I'm out of here but, hey, what other option did I have? Well, running seemed better at that moment, even as Bernard clambered back onto the bonnet and started to suck his robe. Oh, and simpleness isn't a word. Simplicity, that would do. Though I never said that to Duck. Well, in my head I did but not out loud. Didn't want to antagonise him, he may still have a gun.

"You see, he can bring the ducks to us but we need to take him to the ducks. Find their lair and destroy them there."

No, I didn't point out that this rhymed, either.

"We have to confront the devils in their own back yard, confront them, nip them in the bud, ensure their off-spring are not allowed to live, though this may give the option of a sequel that has almost the same plot but different characters. No, we must stop that and stop it soon. *Before it is too late*. Once we were alone, now we have Bernard."

I stopped short of yelling "whoopee" for obvious reasons, well, reasons that were obvious to me.

Our saviour was now licking his wine glass. "Any chance of a refill?" he asked.

"Of course," Duck added, "we will probably perish doing this, as the ducks will put up a fierce fight, but it is a sacrifice worth paying, isn't it?"

Well, I'd stump up a couple of hundred quid if pushed in preference, but, my life, well, if I could get around it…

"We will save the world and that is what we now must do. Well, not now as I have also brought some cheesecake and cream for afters."

"What flavour?"

"Prawn and…"

"Vinegar?"

"Yeauch, no, prawn and vinegar cheesecake? Don't be daft! It's prawn and…"

But before he could end his sentence, Bernard started quaking and shouting "Ducks, ducks, ducks, dusk…" at the top of his voice. "Beware! Beware the ducks!" Then his hand shot out and pointed to the bend in the river.

"To the car," said Duck, "Bernard has given us a warning. Oh and the ducks over there may also be a bit of a hint."

Duck dived into the car, threw it into gear and then switched it on. Then threw it into gear again. The car screeched away from the river and our picnic lay there, half eaten, until the ducks arrived and this delayed their chase. But not for long.

"Should we leave Bernard on the bonnet?" I asked. He was still sitting there, looking to the heavens, oblivious of almost everything.

"He'll be okay, He's a prophet, he'd know if he should get in," Duck replied. And he was right. I wasn't sure if his ability to stay on the bonnet as we whizzed long was a supernatural power or something to do with having his robe caught in the door.

The ducks were on our tail, but Duck kept on driving until we came to a group of picnickers in a small field, where Duck stopped the

141

car and dived out. This was strange as I thought we were trying to escape but, apparently, not so.

"Get out, get out!" shouted Duck to the revelers, "you are in grave danger!"

Everyone turned to look at Duck, tutting and telling their children to "Ignore the mad man with the robed man and the more normal looking man" and carried on normally. Looking around, you could understand their reticence: the sun shone, all was calm with not a duck in sight. The only irritant was the occasional wasp on the chocolate bit of a ninety-niner.

"Where are they? Didn't I see ducks?" asked Duck.

"Yes, I think so... but, you know, maybe I was wrong. Easy mistake to make."

And the silence grew more silent.

And the more silence. Followed by more. Then a little bit more. And more.

Followed by an almighty crash as three ducks smashed into the scene, flying manically, murderously into the heads of the picnicking groups, bowling them into the river, into each other, into the trees, quacking, cackling, killing all, yet leaving Bernard, Duck and myself strangely untouched.

Then silence again. As quickly as they had arrived, they seemed to have gone.

We looked at the carnage in the previously tranquil scene.

Bernard sat upright, pointing.

"Oh, no. He knows. He knows why they left us. They want us to come. They want the final confrontation. And Bernard knows where. Or at least a broad hint of the direction."

Duck said we must go, leaving the carnage, blood and death to the wasps. These buzzed around the ice-creams, as they do. The piercing screams of the people just seconds before stayed in my ears long after we got into the car and drove away from the scene. Perhaps they will reverberate in my head for ever.

Or maybe I'll get over it, like you do.

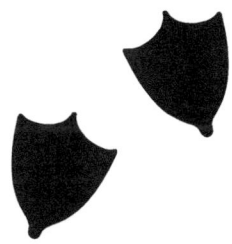

The fishponds had a history. Well, a mythology. It was rumoured that two boys, Donald and his brother, had drowned there on a dark evening some years ago, on this very night. The thirteenth. Obviously.

The fishponds was a dark place when the sun was down, scary, uninviting, mysterious, dank, smelly and not the place for a date. But Joe, Mike and Sheila didn't care; they wanted to try themselves or, more specifically, try Sheila out, for they had dared her and she, silly teenager, had called the bluff of the two spotty classmates and now she was beginning to wonder why.

"We'll video it all," said Joe.

"Cool dude!" shouted Mike.

"Grow up and be English," Sheila commented though she felt ill at ease as they slid their way down the bank and towards the fishponds. It was just getting cold. "You don't scare me, you know." Though actually they did, just not in the way they wanted to scare her.

"So, where are you?" she shouted. But they did not reply. They were now quietly hanging from a tree, upside down, dangling dead in the breeze as a small group of ducks sat around silently waiting for their next victim. But they would have to wait.

"Dudes, eh?" said Sheila. "Ha, so grown up but any chance of some casual sex, no, too busy playing music and growing spots, horrible little oinks. Honestly, I have to get a life..."

And a stray ducks flashed across her scalp, missing her completely and crashing noiselessly into a tree. The ducks captured this on Joe and Mike's video, for posterity and Duck Tube.

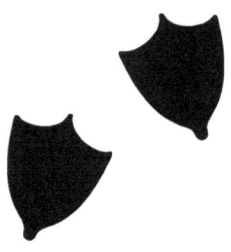

TEN

"Come on, little duckies, come on," encouraged the small grey-haired lady who stood at the edge of the lake in the fading evening light, a small brown bag in her hands.

"Come on."

The little old lady was old and red-bonneted, slightly frail looking and diminutive in stature. She had unusually large feet for such a fragile body which protruded from a large grey, army-style overcoat. If anyone had have viewed her now in the declining light, they would only see an old woman who was wiling away her twilight years by giving comfort to the wild animals who roamed the local woods and lakes and who she now took to her heart as a sop to the cruel world that no longer seemed to understand their appeal. A cold, uncaring world where, unless you had a role, you had no future. This was an easy misconception to have about Mrs. Merganser and an easy one to make.

It was a misconception the Park warden made.

He was responsible for Health & Safety and had an ego to inflate, so when he approached her, his concern was for the little lady herself. So it was a surprise to receive the sharp and very painful kick to his shins from her red Wellington boots, sized eleven.

"Ouch!" he said as he held his shin and did a little dance. "Why did you do that? I was just trying to keep you from the edge of this very dangerous lake... not to mention the ducks. We know what they've done all over the country, they could do the same to you..."

"Shut yer face," she said, throwing more crusts of bread into the lake.

"But..." he started.

He did not continue.

His words were taken from him.

In the distance he could see three mallards gliding effortlessly towards Mrs. Merganser and himself. Hopping gracelessly, he decided

145

not to argue with her or her red Wellington boots but, for safety's sake, headed for his handily placed Warden's Hut where he thought he'd be safe. He locked the door behind himself and crawled under the table.

"Come on, little duckies, come on, here's food, here's some food."

The ducks, almost smiling, silently swam closer and closer.

They stopped just short of the bank of the lake, under the serene shadow of the oak tree at the edge, framed in the darkening light. They eyed their quarry and the bread crusts. As an appetiser, they started on the crusts floating on the water, ready to take their human quarry later.

"Come on duckies," Mrs. Merganser continued.

And then there was a large bang, a flash and down flurried into the evening sky as Mrs. Merganser took the bomb from her brown bag and blew the three ducks into oblivion.

As the Warden unlocked his hut and ran out, all he could see was the floating bodies of three ducks, a small ripple in the water and the receding and slightly mad cackle of a woman disappearing into the night.

It took a great deal to recover from the shock of the attack we had witnessed; fourteen pints of warm lager left me shaken and still stirred. Duck sat, drinking martinis and tomato juice (with a hint of asparagus) in silence, scratching his head with his one hand which meant he spilled quite a bit of tomato juice and martini. Bernard, meantime, was outside of the Portcullis & Unicycle pub, still attached to the bonnet of the car, refusing to move (and unable to do so as his robe was stuck in the grill at the front).

"It is a sacred garment, do not try to remove it, you may tear it and then all the goodness will be gone. Then we will be doomed!" he said.

"Shall be doomed, isn't it?" I corrected.

"Shall, will, may, who cares! Do not move the robe!" he replied, quaking visibly.

So we didn't. Duck noted he could be there, on the bonnet, for some time at this rate. So he ordered another round.

We sat at the bar, leaving Bernard outside, thinking and drinking though not necessarily in that order. We were alone with our thoughts of total world destruction, apart from the cheery landlord who kept smiling and serving us, the only people in the pub.

"It's been a bit quiet, I have to admit. Takings are on the dodgy side," he told us. "Must be to do with them ducks. Legend has it around here that... but that's not a duck thing. More to do with sheep as I recall. Still, maybe they're interchangeable. Aren't they?" he continued, absent-mindedly.

"What legend is that?" I asked, slurring a little.

"That the world will end if, erm, that a woman will rule when....no, that's not right. Oh, yes, that, oh, no, that's not it either. Anyway, legend has it... that's all I know."

He decided to leave it at that.

"I am not moving until I can remove my sacred garment!" shouted Bernard from outside.

"Whatever," replied Duck in a manner that suggested that he, too, was shaken by our ordeal.

"But maybe it had something to do with sheep or ducks or... oh, no that wasn't it. Or was it? A Welsh man. Yes, a Welsh man. When a Welsh man is seen."

The bar went silent. Well, it was pretty silent but it went more silent as Duck and I looked at the barman.

"A Welsh man?" I asked.

"Yes, I think, a Welsh man. Or was it a guy called Welsh? Or Walsh. Mike Walsh? No. No, I think it was a Welsh man. How did it go now? *When the Welsh man this way comes, better get off your fat Yorkshire bums.* I think that's how it went. I think that was it. Could have been Walsh I suppose. Or Feltz."

"I will not get off of this bonnet come hell or high water!" shouted Bernard.

Ten minutes later we were back at the house, Duck bolting doors and Bernard looking slightly confused.

"Was that hell or high water?" he asked.

"Neither, it was me," answered Duck, "as I needed to save you. And me. Oh, and him. I think they are closing in on us. The barman gave us a clue. His last words, of course."

The three ducks moved in on the house.

They spotted an open window and were in.

Markus was ordering a taxi.

"Yes, I must be going home to Helsinki so I am needing a taxi to be taking me to the airport. Please be with me by the hour as I am late."

He was very stereotypically Finnish and also very tall. Seven foot two, by all accounts. Which made life in the small Yorkshire cottage tricky, as he spent most of his time either crouched or ducked.

And that was ironic, as the three ducks flew at him but missed, flying out of the window opposite and straight into a large container lorry that just happened to be passing.

Markus' cab came and he returned safely to Finland. And the ducks never new how close they came to The Big Finnish.

Once content that he was safe, Duck sat down and scratched his head again. He did not look happy. The house was shrouded in an impending silence, a silence of doom, the noiselessness only broken by the loud ticking of the grandfather clock in the corner of the dining room and the sound of Bernard singing "The Green, Green Grass of Home" (at least a version of it) in the bathroom. It was a sullen scene. And the noise wasn't up to much, either.

Almost overcome by a leaden feeling, I informed Duck that I was going stir crazy and needed to go out for a walk. This made Duck jump into the air in an agitated manner.

"A walk! No, are you crazy? A walk? It will be a walk you never come back from, like Scott of the Antarctic!"

"That was Oates, wasn't it?" I corrected.

"Whatever," replied Duck which I wished he'd stop saying. "Look, you can't go out! Ouch! I wish I wouldn't shout like that, it really hurts. Anyway, look, it's dangerous out there, there are ducks out there determined to kill and maim but mostly kill all humans in their effort to control this world of ours. They are close to achieving this aim and we need you to help us two, the only hope for civilisation's survival."

"Me? I'm needed?"

"Yes, you've got a credit card and our credit level is, well, not very good. We can't stop them without money. And now they have a quarry."

I looked amazed at this. Not because of the credit card but I wondered why they'd need a quarry, what they would be quarrying and how they would drive a fork lift truck and other related mechanical diggers.

"Do you know what a quarry is?" asked Duck.

"Yes, it's a …"

"No, in this case it's an individual, a target, the one person they need to help achieve their aim."

"That's what I was going to say…"

"Liar, you thought it was large area used to mine stuff and the like with mechanical diggers, didn't you?"

"Might have."

"Well it's not, well, okay, it can be but in this case the quarry I was referring to was, in fact, Bernard."

There was a silence punctuated by the quarter of an hour striking from the clock.

"Really?"

"Yes, it really is Bernard!"

"No, I meant is it really quarter past? Time passes so slowly when your life is in mortal danger!"

Duck looked at me.

"Yes," he carried on regardless, "Bernard is the quarry as he is the ONLY one who can stop the total destruction of this world by these ducks. Nobody will listen to us, though I know we haven't tried too many people, but they wouldn't listen anyway, so it's up to us, me, you and him to stop them. And here's me with a terrible migraine."

"Yes," I said, "but couldn't I just do once around the garden, I'm just getting a little bit bouncing off the walls at the moment a bit of fresh air and…"

"No!! Has nothing I said made any sense to you at all?"

"Is that a rhetorical question?"

"We are doomed unless the three of us, me, Bernard and your credit card, stay alive. We cannot afford to lose you and should you venture outside now that is just what we may do. And I cannot afford that to happen. Afford, get it?"

I could not tell him that the ducks' real quarry was, in fact, him. Well, it would have been unfair as he had such a migraine. So I let him go to the kitchen and shove his head under the cold water tap though

I'd have thought an aspirin would have been less problematical and you don't bang your head on an aspirin like you can on a tap. As he did.

"Ow! That doesn't help."

There was a silence.

"It's too quiet," said Duck.

"Don't knock it, Bernard's stopped his terrible warbling, I used to like that song, too..."

We looked at each other meaningfully. Then we raced upstairs to the bathroom. In the cold water lay the still body of Bernard, submerged and lifeless, it seemed. The bathroom window was slightly ajar and, in the breeze, we could just make out a couple of duck feathers floating in the breeze.

We exchanged meaningful glances.

"So, our last hope has gone," said Duck.

"No," I replied, "he is not our last hope. You are."

It came on the place like a flash flood. Within minutes, the remnants of the area were running, running to be away from the ravages of the killers that had descended upon them, hanging onto their lives that now hung by a gossamer like thread from a crumbling cliff edge.

The remaining, surviving few flooded into the large warehouse-like warehouse building, which was actually a warehouse, on the edge of the small city. All types of people: school children, bankers, cyclists, nuns, traffic wardens, teachers, detectives, young singles, families, gays, lesbians, people who swung both ways, ship's mates, retired footballers, grocers, babes in arms (and buggies), twitchers, Big Issue sales people, journalists, shop assistants, librarians, chartered accountants, bakers, the unemployed, biographers, prostitutes, local councillors, failed businessmen, orators, farmers, fishmongers, chandlers, electricians, pot holers, short hand typists, more teachers, opticians, VAT inspectors, florists, research scientists, gypsies, tennis coaches, dentists, refuse and disposal engineers, lollipop women, telephone sales operatives, shepherds (with sheep), shepherds (without sheep), supervisors, crime investigators, animal trainers, trapeze artists, chartered surveyors, farriers, croupiers, cartographers, licensed taxi drivers, navel gazers, victualers, day care assistants and many more... but strangely, not one plumber.

They had all congregated at the large warehouse-like warehouse for shelter from the hurricane of ducks that had suddenly descended on their small city (so named even though it didn't have a cathedral or university), leaving the emergency services overwhelmed and unprepared for this eventuality: total devastation.

They, the emergency services that is, had been trying to cope with some small isolated incidents in the early afternoon when a large dark cloud of ducks had descended from the skies like the rain of death, destroying the infrastructure, setting light to buildings, massacring innocent and not so innocent people, bringing dread and fear to all who survived and even those who didn't.

The skies blackened with the evil wings of death and within minutes the city was almost no more. It was devastating, efficient and ruthless. And surprisingly quick. Few survived; they may not have been the lucky ones as they were now congregated in the large warehouse-like warehouse waiting to find out their fate from the local constabulary, now singularly represented by one PC 452 who stood alone and ashen faced at the front of the people in the large warehouse-like warehouse, calling for silence and hoping to give some glimmer of hope to the small mass of humanity gathered together in fear in the large warehouse-like warehouse that was now their one and only sanctuary from the devils they once called ducks.

He once again called for silence and this time it fell immediately, like a cow pat onto the dewy morning grass.

"Ladies and gentlemen," he began, before remembering his diversity training and adding, "and anybody else that is excluded by those terms," at which point a sheep bleated his thanks, "but we are in the deep shambi here. According to my sources, we have no sources. We currently have no telephone connection, either landline or mobile, and every other known communication medium has been lost to us, so nobody knows about our situation and we can't tell them about our current position. Which doesn't look good. As we can see from BBC News 24..." and he looked across the large warehouse-like warehouse to a large screen on the wall of the large warehouse-like warehouse which was showing the news. It reported.

"And in further developments, a small city that has no cathedral or university was laid waste today by The Ducks. A spokesperson for the small city said that they were in 'the deep shambi' and that there were few survivors. Those who did survive are apparently stuck in a large warehouse-like warehouse at the edge of the city with little hope of being rescued or ever having a university or cathedral built now. But, on a lighter note now, over to Stephanie for the weather. Steph, how's it looking out there...?"

"Thanks, George."

PC 452 gave his "I told you so face" and wondered what to do next.

The crowd fell silent, though they had been silent before. Maybe they fell more silent, if that is possible. Any way, there was no noise.

"Well, I've locked the large warehouse-like warehouse doors, so we should be..." he started to say only to be interrupted by a huge noisy banging at the doors of the large warehouse-like warehouse.

The crowd stayed silent, save for a few screams and one shout of "Flipping heck! What was that?" and a short bleat from a sheep.

PC 452 looked at the door in horror.

There was another loud noisy banging.

The crowd gasped, more women screamed, some children started to cry, sheep bleated and teeth chattered. Then silence again.

Another huge noisy bang.

And another.

"Shall I open the door?" asked a man, turning the large handle.

"No!!!" screamed PC 452 but he was too late.

The door swung open.

There was a gasp.

An awed silence followed.

"Oh, look," said PC452, "it's a small boy with a cap and a large broom. Come on in, silly boy."

And the small boy with the cap and a large broom entered the large warehouse-like warehouse to a huge sigh of relief.

"Now, close those doors and, as I was saying..." started PC452 to be interrupted immediately again by another large noisy bang at the door.

The crowd gasped, more women screamed, some children started to cry, more teeth chattered and another sheep, or maybe it was the same one, bleated. Then a resounding silence.

Another huge noisy bang.

And another.

"Have you got a brother with a cap and a large broom?" asked PC 452 of the small boy but, before he could answer, the huge doors flew open and another small boy with a cap and a large broom walked in.

"That's my twin brother," said the first small boy.

There was a collective sigh of relief.

"Now," started PC 452 again, "oh, close those doors, will you, now what I..." but he was again interrupted by a large noisy banging at the doors of the large warehouse-like warehouse doors.

"Shall I open it, PC McGarry?" asked the man. "He may have another brother!"

PC 452 thought about this. Triplets was a bit of a long shot. Though it could be a younger or even older brother.

But before he could gather his thoughts and say no, there was another large noisy bang and the doors flew open and huge numbers of ducks flooded into the large warehouse-like warehouse to finish off their job of killing all of the remaining residents of the small city, gathered in the large warehouse-like warehouse, which would now definitely never have a cathedral or a university.

After seventeen minutes of mayhem, dead bodies lay all around the large warehouse-like warehouse. No-one was saved. Not even the small boys with caps or even their brooms.

The ducks, happy with their work, contentedly viewed the scene of carnage, gave themselves a few congratulatory clucks, then flew off into the dark black skies through the large warehouse-like warehouse doors, looking to bring death and destruction to the rest of the country as soon as possible.

Silence fell over the scene.

Then BBC News 24 crackled back into life.

"Breaking news from a small city in the North of England," said George. "Erm, strange, this just cryptically says, No-one survived. Save for a small monkey."

And as he said this, a small monkey skipped across the dead, looking for fruit and car keys.

"And, on a lighter note now, over to Stephanie for another weather update. How's it looking out there, Steph?"

"Well, George, not too good in the North..."

We dashed along the winding, leafy roads towards the hospital with Bernard's lifeless body in tow.

"Would it have been quicker to use the car?" I asked, so we went back and got the car.

Using the car rather than our feet, we reached the hospital in under twenty minutes. When we got there, we saw a scene of mayhem. And we couldn't park because the parking meters weren't working and we didn't want to get fined by not paying and displaying. Others weren't so choosy; there were hundreds of cars, abandoned by their desperate owners looking for some shelter and support from the terror of the ducks.

It was chaos.

As we approached the hospital, people were stretched out over the well manicured lawns (it was a private hospital) with people spilling all over the hedgerows and beautiful floral displays. Duck and I stopped in astonished amazement.

The noisy, bustling and mostly bleeding crowd were being kept in order by two blood-spattered doctors who were forming orderly queues and shouting "Look, you will all be seen but *NOT* if you don't make an orderly queue well... erm, just make a queue will you and if you could try *NOT* to bleed on the grass, that would help, too."

"It says don't walk on the grass, no mention of not bleeding on it," said a bleeder.

"Don't be so pedantic," pleaded the doctor.

Small fights were breaking out in the queues as people jostled for position and there was a genuine feeling of danger. Duck stared at me and we did not feel safe. But then, using then tension of the moment and with a determined look on his face, he headed defiantly towards the two doctors with me in tow, ignoring shouts of "Hey, you've just arrived!, "Get to the back", "He looks quite well to me!" and "You're not even bleeding!".

The first doctor, a young man with an untidy mop of ginger hair, the red blood glistening on his starched white coat in the sunshine, approached us, smiling, yet shaking his head in a confident manner.

"Now, look, I don't want to start trouble here but you really must keep in the queue…" he started but was interrupted by Duck who informed him that we didn't want medical attention but just wanted the answer to a couple of questions.

"What are these people doing here?"

"Bleeding mostly," he replied without a hint of humour, "and over our grass and gravel. It'll be a bugger to get out, blood always is. Oh, and you," he shouted at a man who had half of his head missing, "you, try to direct the blood onto other people, will you. People wash up better than gravel!"

"Yes, but what happened?" asked Duck.

"You're not reporters are you?" he asked, suspiciously.

"No!" we replied, indignantly.

"Pity, I've got some good photos of this lot that I thought would make good front page news stuff. Worth a bob or two, I reckon. Oh, sorry, yes, what happened? Well, some sort of attack. Not humans, though, some animal attack, we think. Strange, most people didn't quite know what hit them but some were muttering about ducks. Ducks? Seems mad to me. Erm, do you have a body there?"

"Oh, yes. This is Bernard. Or was," I helpfully intersected.

"Don't you know about the duck attacks sweeping the country?" asked an incredulous Duck.

"Quite frankly, no, we're private, mostly beer and skittles here, the real world's not for us. Ducks, you say? Bit weird that. Ducks aren't normally aggressive world domineering types, are they? Would you like to bury him?"

"Bernard?" I asked.

"But it is ducks," Duck confirmed.

The queue stopped pushing and shoving at this point. There was a silence that fell on all.

"Yes," shouted one man with a badly mauled set of legs, "ducks, that's it! Ducks! Devil ducks, intent on the death and destruction of mankind!"

"Ducks!" cried another "Ducks from another planet!"

"Cannibal ducks!" cried yet another.

"Well, technically, no, they would be ducks who ate other ducks," corrected another as he tried to stem the blood from his bitten off arm.

"Bloody teacher," muttered another.

"I'm a lecturer, actually," corrected the other.

"But there were ducks. Huge swarms of them!"

"I'm not sure a collective noun is a swarm. A paddling, I think, if on water, or a team or a raft or a plump but never a swarm. That's just bees."

"What's the collective noun for a lot of pillocks?"

"But there's only me so, technically..."

"So, technically, shut up, pillock!"

"Oh, yes. Okay."

Duck looked at the doctor and then the sky.

"Can I just give you some of words of advice young man?" he asked the doctor.

"Well, yes," he replied. "As long as it's not medically based as I do have a degree and..."

"No, it's quite simple advice, really," Duck continued.

"Okay," replied the nice doctor.

"Run. Run like the bloody wind," suggested Duck, pointing to the skies.

"But my patients!" asked the doctor.

"Your patients may be running out!" shouted Duck as he dropped Bernard's body, pulled my arm and ran off into the distance as a huge shadow covered the hospital grounds just as a large amount of ducks converged on the bleeding masses.

We heard the screams as we ran on.

We did not turn to look.

Not many were saved.

Luckily, we were the only two survivors. But for how long?

I leant across the bed and felt her slim, tender body against mine. I couldn't quite recall what her name was or who she was but it had been hectic recently and all I knew was that she smelt like a woman should smell. I ran her auburn hair through my fingers and she sighed a little as I moved my other hand towards her pink flesh and down her thigh and then she melted, like a pat of butter on a hot summer's day.

"Oi!!" interrupted Duck, "Less of that!"

"Oh, no, not another dream?" I asked.

"Yes, another dream," Duck pointed out. "Pity, we could have done with some gratuitous sex to brighten stuff up at this juncture, but, unfortunately, it's not that sort of book."

I groaned.

"And you can cut that out, too," Duck barked.

ELEVEN

The large man, dressed in a dirty Parker with a fedora hat on his bulging shaven head and a man bag around his shoulders, sweatily and breathlessly pushed into the large cavernous cavern. He'd been on the trail of the missing piece of Mother Shipton's manuscript for many a day now, driven by a desire to rid the country of the menace of the ducks, and the trail had brought him here, to Knaresborough and Mother Shipton's cave. A blindingly obvious choice, when you come to think of it, especially since he'd realised that only Mother Shipton's prophesies may hold the key to the current problem, but it wasn't one that immediately jumped out at our explorer friend, who doesn't need to be named as he won't be here for long.

Having said that, about coming to Knaresborough and Mother Shipton's cave, that is (as that part was quite poorly written) in his geographical defence he had started his quest for the missing piece of the manuscript in Barbados which, whilst being many miles off track, is somewhat more attractive and a great deal warmer than Knaresborough. You may damn him for being an obviously poor explorer but you have to praise his choice of holiday destinations.

Anyway, back to the plot.

He scuttled along the dark cavernous cavern on his hands and knees, mostly for dramatic effect but also because he was slightly over-weight and a little tired. He had found, through his endless research, that Mother Shipton had prophesised many things: that there would be horseless carriages, that there would be a fire in London, that men would walk under water and that the world would end in 1881, amongst other less remarkable guesses. He therefore agreed with common folklore that although slightly deluded, maybe she did have a power for prophesy which, if they'd had The Lottery back in the fifteenth century, she may have used for her own ends rather than for the good of the world. There was a perpetual rumour in prophesising circles that there was a missing page in her manuscript and that that missing piece, the piece that would fill in the jigsaw puzzle of the terrible times the country in, was actually here in Knaresborough and not, strangely, in Barbados, Cuba, Brazil, Australia or the other warmer, more exotic and, let's face it, more photogenic places around the world that he'd just visited. Just on his doorstep, in fact, well, since he lived in Greaseborough that wasn't technically true but it was close enough for jazz.

He'd found the original cave which had been the home to the orphan Ursula Sontheil in the late 15th century quite easily (the brown tourist signpost helped) and he'd smuggled himself into it after the straggling few late sightseers had left. Hiding behind a curtained screen, he slipped out, checking that everyone had gone (and there had only been three visitors that day), and eyed the small room/cave that had been Ursula's house for most of her life. He looked around and saw a small tunnel like opening just to the right of the rough hewn table that was propped against the wall. Checking no-one was around, he crept over and peered in. The tunnel itself was dark and low but he could just make out what seemed to be a small glimmer of light at the far end. Maybe this was where the missing piece of the manuscript was; hopefully, as this was more dramatic than just leaving it on the table. He got onto his hands and knees and eased himself into the gap.

He crept along the cave on his hands and knees until he came to the far end where he needed to flop onto his belly to crawl to the small glowing part of the tunnel some feet away from him. He crawled and crawled further into the gloomy cave.

And then, there, in the gloom, he could see, flapping around, a small piece of paper or maybe even parchment, just inches away from his sweaty hands.

This could be it. This could be the missing page, the page that he had been searching for now for most of his adult life. Well, most of the weekend, at any rate. This could be the piece of paper that saved the country, saved the world. He took a deep breath and scrambled to the end of the cavern.

As he breathlessly crawled, he finally reached out and, as he did, the piece of paper undramatically stayed still and he grabbed it first time without any problem whatsoever.

He looked at it, hands trembling.

Would this be the answer, the solution, the holy grail that he thought it to be, the answer to the problem, an insight into the reasons and meaning of the "current situation"?

His hands shook with anticipation as he peered at the small piece of paper through the gloom to see what wonderful, life shattering insight it had.

Here, he thought to himself, could be the answer, the solution to the duck problem, the insight into the whys and wherefores and, yes, he could be the one with *THE* answer in his hand, the missing piece in the bloodied jigsaw puzzle that was the... and a voice in his head said "get on with it".

So, he did. He gazed through the gloom as he carefully unfolded the piece of paper.

And he read the scrawled words on it nervously.

He sighed as he took it all in.

"One less today, please," it read and then, mysteriously, it added "Labrador".

And then he felt a small pain in the back of his head which flicked his fedora off and it fell to the floor, spinning, blood spattered. The ducks had, quietly, claimed another victim after the assassination of the milkman and they had kept the secret of the missing piece of the manuscript. Forever.

She was naked and stood in front of the full length mirror in her bedroom, admiring her beautiful form. At twenty-four she felt close to her peak, a fact that was confirmed by the image that formed in the glass.

A large, toothy smile formed across her deep red lips. No plastic here, all her own work. Her eyes flashed up and down, admiring her own body, taking in the brown beauty of her marble-like skin which had strutted the sun-baked beaches of Brazil in such fine, killing form just nine days earlier.

The longer she looked, the more and more she became sexually aroused at the sight of her own body. She slowly ran her ring-less left hand up and down her browned, tight thighs, moisturising, looking at her own pert breasts, as her right hand massaged the large, erect brown nipples, which flicked and rose with excitement. Her hand cautiously moved up her thigh and she sighed, breathlessly, at the thought of...

She heard a noise downstairs.

"Damn," she whispered to herself, pulling her long, auburn hair into a knotted bun, "damn, damn, damn, damn. Ruin my pleasure, as usual."

Snatching the robe from the king-sized bed and throwing it around her tort body, she caught one last, pleasing glimpse of herself before she tightly knotted the belt around her perfect waistline in annoyance.

She heard the footsteps on the stairs and felt the familiar sick feeling deep down inside that slender, honed stomach.

Thinking quickly, she ran gracefully for the bathroom and, hearing the footsteps coming closer and closer and closer, joyfully slammed the door and pushed the lock across.

Safe, inside, she leant back against the door and breathed a huge, perfect sigh of relief from the depths of her ample bosom. She glanced into the bathroom mirror, ensuring that her hair fell across her face in an alluring manner. Her black eyelashes flickered.

"Erm, hello, it's me, dearest!" came the weak voice from chinless wonder below.

Her perfect face with the graceful cheekbones contorted sharply at the sound of the voice.

"I'm having a bath, darling. Make some tea, there's a dear."

"Shall I come in and..."

"No, no, don't come in, I'm doing, erm, womanly things."

"Oh. Okay."

There was a short silence as she stopped and looked at the empty bath. Quickly, she flicked the taps on and paused only to sprinkle bath salts into the flowing water. This completed, she unknotted her robe, slipped it off and caught a quick glimpse of herself, looking as beautiful as usual, as no doubt Carlos thought when he first saw her naked on the beach in Brazil. Was it Carlos? Was that his name? Something like that, anyway. Foreign. And she let *HIM* see her body. Just as she had never let Ralph do here in sunny Scunthorpe.

She looked into her own deep brown eyes.

Damn, she thought, she didn't want to marry Ralph for his money, but how else could she get it? Was it wrong to do what she was doing? Oh, how could it be when he was so beautiful and thoughtful with a sprinkling of unabashed modesty? Let's face it, without the addition of sterling, Ralph was no great catch. Let's face it, she hated him and the thought of him getting close to her made her flesh creep. She even shuddered as she thought it. Then she thought of their joint cheque account and her platinum credit card and she felt better.

The bath was almost full.

He was old, that was true, but at least that meant that she could spend his money with a clear conscience, not that she had much of a conscience. Though she must have; having sex could kill the dear old moneyed Ralph and she wouldn't let *THAT* happen. That must be love.

So, she just let him get on with the pleasant task of earning money whilst she got on with the task of spending it. After all, how could she have sex with someone she hardly knew? Yes, she could spend his money but sex was a different matter; money was okay, sex was not. She hadn't even let him see her naked yet but they'd only been married two years, so it was early days yet. Not that it was *EVER* going to happen.

Ralph, naïve, ageing, chinless, grey millionaire that he was, was stumped by the behaviour of his new wife, his third. She was different to the other two who had divorced him, taking millions off him, because *she* loved him. The others didn't. Ralph, by the way, was still a virgin. And an idiot.

Okay, he argued to nobody but himself, she was a bit of a slut at times but, hey, weren't they all? His mother, rest her soul, had warned him of this and she was right! She was always right. Okay, so the milkman delivered the milk in a Porsche but it was an ever-changing world and maybe young people do greet each other in that over-friendly way, though, obviously, she'd never greet Ralph in that way, because Ralph was different. He was her husband! He was an idiot.

"Erm, tea, dear?" he asked from outside the bathroom door.

"That's okay, leave it in my bedroom, I'll get it when I'm finished," she replied.

In her bedroom. Not in their bedroom, as there wasn't a "their" bedroom.

She slipped into the bath and the bubbles seeped over her brown breasts. She lay back in contented relief, relief that he had been kept at arm's length, away from her young, slim, nubile, perfect body.

As she looked down at herself, she was unwittingly being viewed by another source. At the end of the bath, hidden by the steam from the hot tap, the strange, pod-like plant twitched a little, its tendrils slowly beginning to edge towards the left foot it so wanted, so needed, so desired.

Stopping, ensuring the large brown eyes of its quarry were shut, the plant slipped its tendrils into the water and down the floor of the bath, close to her skin. It was easy to slip along the floor of the bath, gliding around her body, ready to engulf her, take her, kill her. It stopped, making sure it didn't disturb her.

Not yet, anyway.

"No ducks in there then!" laughed Ralph nervously.

"Ducks? You what?" came the graceless reply.

"Oh, it's just that ducks have been attacking people all over the country. And I know you like your wild life."

"Have you been to the pub?"

"Erm, no, just concerned for you, darling!"

The plant stopped, letting the conversation run its course and noticing her eyes opening in annoyance.

"Sober up!" she complained to the chinless one.

"No, honest, I've seen it in the newspapers, well, those that are still publishing. Ducks. Seems strange to me, ducks aren't normally wild, blood crazed beasts, well, the ones my mum used to keep weren't."

"They were chickens."

"No, we had ducks, honest. Not one of them killed anyone. Well, apart from that wild eyed one we had once, the one with teeth. Or fangs. Wonder what happened to that one?"

As his voice tailed off so the plant, confident that its quarry had no idea of its closeness, feeling that her eyes were closed, edged closer and forever closer.

Ralph fell silent. She was silent. The plant was silent. It was silent.

The tendril made a sharp, incisive movement, snapping around her big toe and attempting to pull her under the hot, steaming, bubbly water.

As the plant strained, she let out a mighty yelp and her firm bottom slid up the bath, away from the plant, pulling it and its pot towards her, launching it into the hot, steaming bath.

"Shit!" she cried.

"Shit!" the plant would have cried if it had the power of speech, as it hit the water.

She looked angrily down as the soil spilt from the pot, floated to the surface of the water and spoiled her bath.

"You okay, dear?" asked Ralph.

"Bog off!" she said as she looked at the mess in the bath and realised, about the same time as the plant, that both she and it were in the wrong story.

We drove for what seemed like hours. Actually, it was hours but my watch had stopped.

I hardly noticed where we were now, where we were headed, indeed, I hardly noticed that I was driving, as I wasn't, Duck was, which maybe explained why we were constantly being followed by police cars as Duck only had one arm and no driving license. I was too concerned with Duck's under-his-breath utterances of "total devastation, murderous beasts, I could murder a pepperoni pizza" to really concentrate.

As dusk settled over the country, the radio gave us news of the Government's nighttime curfew. It also explained how the armed forces had been paralysed by lightening attacks of ducks. It echoed our fears that little or nothing now stood in the way of the ducks, these monstrous beasts, taking over this country of ours. This we were already painfully aware of. Figures quoted on the radio suggested that more than fifteen million people were now dead or hospitalized or at least quite tired following attacks by ducks. Experts estimated that there were now over twenty million ducks of many varieties on this sceptered isle of ours, which soon would not be ours at all.

Could we believe these figures? Who ever knows. The communication up and down the country had been so poor that accurate figures were difficult to get. No change there, then.

There was no comfort from the radio, especially when the newsreader signed off with a cry of "That is all from the newsroom and as we head back to somber music we'd like to say goodnight and HELP!!".

Duck mumbled about being "close to the sauce" though he may have mumbled "close to the source" as we drove along the dark lanes. He spoke of dark feelings of fear, foreboding and death as his empty stomach rumbled incessantly. Then, as we
swung left towards the few lights ahead that announced a small building he yelled "stop!" to which I pointed out that he was actually driving the car, technically, at least.

"Oh, yes," he calmly said as we did a wild emergency stop and my head hit the ceiling of the car.

There was a long silence. Duck looked around and quietly whispered to me.

"The zoo," he whispered.

"I know, I can see the sign. The one that says 'ZOO'. And why are you whispering?" I whispered.

"You started it," he whispered back. "But that's not important. We must go in."

"It's closed. It's after six."

"No, no, it won't be," he whispered back, "I have a feeling in my stomach."

We alighted the car and I followed him over the darkened road and towards the large, black, wrought iron gates of the zoo which, as I had noticed, helpfully had the word "ZOO" above them. The gates, as Duck feared, were open.

"The gates are open," said Duck.

"As you feared," I replied.

Then I stopped.

"Are you sure it's safe? It is night, the gates are open and there may be animals in there. Wild animals."

I could feel myself shaking.

"There may be animals inside? It's a zoo, of course there are…" he replied then stopped. "But maybe there aren't," he added, enigmatically.

"I don't feel safe," I quivered.

"No, neither am I too. I feel a great sense of real fear, foreboding and maybe just a little pang of hunger. But it is our duty to save this country from the threat of ducks and to save this country from that threat we may have to go into this zoo."

"Ah, may have to. We don't really have to then?" I asked in a kind of corrective manner.

"We have to. We may be terrified, we may be quaking, we may have a small fear for our own well being but, for the good of mankind, for the future of this island, nay, this planet, we need to be brave and strong and go in. You must understand that. So, you go first," and he pushed me through the gates.

"Why me first?" I asked in a pathetically whiney voice.

"Well, you know, I'm kind of more important, aren't I?"

"But…"

"Oh, don't be a sissy, get in," and he shoved me again as he drew his revolver from his pocket, "and I'll just wait outside here in the car where it's safe."

It took a lot of pleading and crying from me plus a little bit of hanging onto his coat and refusing to move to convince Duck that he should stay with me. In the end, he came with me, though from the rear, with revolver at the ready.

There was a noise.

"What was that?" I asked.

"Probably you whingeing, I reckon," came the uncaring reply. "Sissy," he added as he lifted the revolver to shoulder level and aimed

169

over my head mouthing "Don't move" as he did so. I didn't, save for my right knee cap which trembled louder than my bottom lip.

Then there was another noise.

The large gates suddenly creaked open. There was sudden, dull thud. There, under the gates, was the body of a... we knew not what.

"Is it dead?" I asked Duck.

Duck leant over the human body and recoiled in horror.

"Any you guys got any money," the body said, "out of drink down here!"

Against our better judgment, we lifted the huge frame of the prone man, dragged him into the darkened zoo and plonked him onto a wooden bench. He smiled, hiccupped and belched at us through his gapped teeth. He smelt. Really stinky, alcohol stinky. Not pleasant stinky, really smelly, stinky, horrible, bad toilet smelly. He also held a party eight pack in his hand and a tiny notebook in the other. A stub of a cigarette hung from his unshaven face as his eyes rolled lazily around his head as he tried to keep his balance on the bench.

"Haven't got a can opener on you, perchance?" he asked.

We answered in the negative.

"Well, if you haven't, you cannot join me in a drink. Pre-lunch, of course."

"Lunch? It's night time," I corrected.

"Not in my world, squire. Hey, more than one way to skin a monkey. I can get this open."

And he punched a hole in the top of the large can. Duck and I looked on in shocked amazement, whilst holding our noses against the stench.

"There," he said, "care for some, gents? Party Special, nice and warm, quality stuff. Oh, sorry, didn't introduce myself. Bob Whimbrel, Special Reporter, North Yorkshire Daily Bugle. Have pen, will report. That's my line. Made that up myself. But, look, don't tell anyone about this," he added as he took a swig of his drink, "very hush-hush, you know. Secret squirrel stuff. Government don't know. Nobody knows. Not sure if I know. After this I won't! Ha-ha!!"

Duck looked at me. "At first I thought it might have been a dead gorilla," he said. "On second viewing, maybe it is."

"No gorillas here, mate. No animals at all. Gorillas? Those Australian things with pouches? Or is that penguins. No, they're bird things, aren't they. Yes. Write that down, Bob, could be useful. Anyway, no penguins, either. They've gone, the gorillas have gone. As have the giraffes. Gone all gone."

"All gone?" echoed Duck.

"Oh, yes," Bob Whimbrel replied, earnestly, "gone, gone, disappeared, run off, vamoosed, gone, vanished, erm, gone. Wish I had my Thesaurus thing."

Duck looked puzzled.

"All of the animals from the zoo have gone? Who took them?"

"Took them? Don't know, tried asking the zoo keeper but he was dead so wasn't answering. Neither were the other dead people, which you do understand, I mean, I wouldn't talk to anyone if I was dead. Not unless the money was good. And it is when I'm doing the reporting!"

Duck and I looked at each other, as we had done numerous times before and would no doubt do many times to come yet as there were at least forty pages to go, and looked stumped. This also wasn't new. Though this time the stumped look was as stumped as it had been. This time, it looked very stumped indeed. Truly stumped.

Bob Whimbrel looked worse, mind, though he was still able to get most of his drink into his mouth as he talked.

"Never really drank before until they put me on this story. Blimey, it's been bad. With all these dead people I've hardly had a chance to get to the off-license."

Duck asked him to tell us all as we walked through the zoo. He agreed, as long as we held him up on both sides and occasionally emptied drink into his mouth. So, we did.

The zoo was deserted, dark and eerie yet strangely unthreatening. There were no signs of life anywhere.

"So," Bob Whimbrel started up, "when we were told about this stuff, ducks and that, but we thought it was a wind up. We get crank calls all the time. Actually, sometimes it's me phoning, trying to get myself out of the office. But this time it wasn't me. And it wasn't a wind up. So, me and the staff photographer, Clicks Nixon, ha-ha, came down here."

"You have photographs?"

"Oh, yes, we have. There was this brunette, feeding the monkeys and one of the little blighters went over and…"

"No, you got photos of these ducks?" Duck asked, exasperated.

"The ducks? No, not really. Clicks got carried away…"

"With the brunette…" Duck sighed.

"No, he should be so lucky. No, by a duck, well, two of them, to be fair. Picked him up, just flew off with him as the others came in and just kind of reeked havoc. Took everybody out, just like all over the country. No-one was saved."

"Save for you?" Duck asked.

"Oh, yes, good point. I survived. Wonder why?"

Duck and I looked, held our noses and wondered why, too. Maybe the ducks had some taste, after all.

"Bloody miracle, I reckon. Still, no-one can save us now, or so the BBC says and, let's face it, you can't argue with them and Lord Reith. So, we're all doomed. No one can save us. May as well have another drink."

"One person can," Duck said.

"No, it's a party can, actually but, in this case, it is a one person party can!!" laughed Bob Whimbrel.

There was an agonizing silence as he flushed the remains of the can down his throat and then broke the dark silence of the zoo with a deafening, echoing belch.

"Oops, manners! Better out than in, though. So, you see the news is all bad. And it's hitting our circulation, all this death, worse that the internet. Sorry, did you say one person can?"

Duck nodded.

"Good. I have an idea," Bob Whimbrel suggested.

"What is it?" I asked.

"Don't know, forget. Oh, yes, do ducks like beer?"

"What's that in your notebook?" asked Duck.

"Erm, this? Don't know, it's all in short hand. I can write it, but I can't read it. Bloody stupid concept."

"I can read shorthand," said Duck, grabbing the notebook. "This says GO TO THE PUB. How does that help?"

"Does for me," added Whimbrel. "Sounds a good idea at any time. And the barman's currently dead, so it's all free."

Duck tutted and walked away, peering into a nearby cage. The bars had been prized apart with obvious violence; the cage was now empty of the hyenas it had once housed. Duck carefully ran his fingers up and down the bent bars, held his fingers to his nose, smelt the scent and grimaced.

"What do you think?" I asked.

"I think," said Duck, slowly, "that hyenas are dirty little animals. That's horrible. Why do that on the bars?"

"Well, they'll be stopped soon," slurred Bob Whimbrel.

Duck and I looked at the drunken lump of journalism.

"Stopped!" yelled Duck. "Stopped? Are you stupid? We can't stop these creatures! The beasts are at their peak. They are close to their quarry, they are close to their target and they know it. Look around you man. They are killing their own now. They started on humans but now they're doing it for fun. Killing, maiming, slicing, dicing, eating, devouring, nothing is sacred to these devil beasts. They even killed the king of the jungle. That's how confident they are. They know no fear. They do not fear man but know only man stands in their way now. They are determined to destroy mankind and win over the entire planet. And they will, unless..."

"Unless what?" I asked.

"Did they kill the armadillos?" asked Bob Whimbrel.

"Sorry?" asked an incredulous Duck.

"The armadillos? Did they kill them? I like armadillos. And they have armour. What, they have armour and they killed them? We've had it then," slurred Bob Whimbrel.

"Unless?" I repeated to Duck.

"Sorry?"

"You said unless a few paragraphs back. Unless what?"

"Unless? I don't rightly know. They have come here to do what they have come to do and they seem to have been very successful. They have even killed other animals. They are, at the moment, unstoppable. A large killing machine. They cannot be stopped, unless..."

"There you go again!"

"Unless we can find out why. If we can find their lair, if we can find their motivation, we may have a chance. Of course, we may not have a chance at all. I'm not too sure any more. They may never be stopped. But it's up to us to stop them..."

"What, me?" asked Bob Whimbrel.

"No, luckily, not you, just us..."

"Good."

"...to stop them. We are alone in knowing what they know and they know that we know that we may not know enough but we may know enough to let them know that we know enough to stop them knowing what we think we know that they think they don't know."

"I'll drink to that," said Bob Whimbrel.

I looked confused but in a caring way.

"So, we'd better get on," added Duck.

"Okay if I stay here?" asked Bob Whimbrel. "Got the front page to do. Can't quite get a handle on what the headline should be yet.

Ducks Run Amok In Zoo. Bit Daily Telegraph that. *Ducks Eat Things*. No, that's not working, either. *Ducks Cause Global Warning (sic)*. Bit Guardian that. *Bars In Knaresborough Closed. Ducks Blamed*. Now, that makes more sense to me and it will grab the locals. Well, the few locals who are still alive. *Zoo Ducks TerroriseDrugged Supermarket Staff*. Like that one. Brings a local flavour with scandal."

Bob Whimbrel hadn't noticed that we had already left.

As we got back into the car, we heard a large cry and an even larger thud. Either Bob Whimbrel had been killed by a duck or he'd run out of beer and fell off the bench. The second option was probably the right one but, right now, we had other things on our mind.

"Time for the big finish," Duck said, dramatically.

In the large park, the wind yet again swept around the brown leaves, pushing and pulling them into the cold night air, as another young couple, though very similar to a couple you've read about before, walked hand-in-hand in the failing light, desperately trying to stare into each others' eyes in the gathering gloom, though ultimately failing.

Saying nothing to each other, their body language speaking more volumes than mere words that I can write here, they carelessly strode on down the grassy bank towards the lake. As they reached the bank, they stopped and exchanged a swift kiss, their legs brushing the longer grass that grew up from the edge of the lake. Unaware of the danger which still lurked, they smiled and walked on along the sensuous curve of the bank.

Behind one of the moored rowing boats, that only months before had been this very couples' love boat, sat a fat mallard, its beak still dripping blood from a recent kill. As it heard the humans approach, it held its breath, smelling the air for the approaching smell of human flesh.

The young man looked about and thought the entire thing smelled familiar.

So, he leant over and pretended to do his shoe up.

And, when she wasn't looking, he leaped up and made a run for it.

And he got out alive. Again. Though this time, it was forever.

Okay, so it may have been Sunday, there may have been tourists but unfortunately needs must.

They'd left hints, they'd looked at the skies and fallen over, they'd even paddled around their feeding bowls like ducks to give their feeders a hint but enough was enough. Outside, they heard a huge noise on the Thames and the crumbling of bricks on Tower Bridge, along with the screaming of the victims.

Bran looked at the others.

"Time to go, boys," he said, clearly and they all upped and flew away from the impending doom of the humans in the Tower.

The Beefeaters looked an, aghast but knowing their fate was now sealed. The ravens had spoken, literally.

TWELVE

As dawn broke, we found ourselves on the Great North Road, as it isn't known, heading who knows where. There were no cars to be seen; indeed little stirred at all, save for the occasional fires from the hastily assembled camp-sites in the surrounding fields by the few remaining survivors from the onslaught of the ducks. The inhabitants of Yorkshire, hearing the stories of the ducks, headed for the country in the hope that the old adage of safety in numbers would be true. Though maybe it would just give the ducks a bigger target.

We stopped at a deserted filling station and I started to fill the car, or at least the petrol tank part of it, nervously looking over my shoulder for any signs of ducks. There were none, just the signs of duck rampage: broken windows, deserted cars and open packets of barbeque briquettes on the forecourt. Well, I assumed that was down to the ducks but you never know. The cold wind whistled around the pumps, blowing yesterday's newspapers around the forecourt, playing around my ankles with the discarded sweet wrappers of earlier forages.

"Hurry up," Duck shouted, from the safety of the car, "it's bloomin' cold in here!"

"I'm trying to get it to the exact pound here," I said, "and it just keeps ticking over to the extra penny. I can't stand that!"

"Yes, well, you may notice a severe lack of cashier," Duck correctly pointed out.

"Oh, yes," I sheepishly responded as a front page circled the car and wrapped itself around the car aerial. The headline caught my eye: "Nude Paedophile Vicar Killed in Launderette by Ducks" it screamed.

Another newspaper flapped around the forecourt three times and then landed, ominously, on the petrol pump in front of me.

"Horror gripped the country again yesterday," it read, "as there were more reports of vicious attacks on the residents of many Yorkshire towns and cities. After the terrible destruction of most cities

177

in the south and midlands, the terror has slipped up the country as ducks have started to descend on the north of England. In one incident, our reporter Bob Whimbrel reports, an alleged pedophile vicar got his alleged comeuppance from, ironically, an alleged young duck that flapped him to death in a local launderette. Local residents said 'Serves him right, child molester' before adding 'Watch out, bloody ducks!'. The Government has declared a state of emergency and has suspended all television broadcasts. Racing at Doncaster will go ahead as planned."

I was no longer shocked at this news, but my feet were now getting wet and beginning to smell of petrol.

"Hurry up," shouted Duck, "they could attack at any time!"

I looked around at the desolate scene. All around the dark clouds crowded the sloping hills into a menacing pose. I replaced the pump and climbed slowly onto Duck's knee.

"Erm, if you don't mind, I'll drive," Duck commented.

"Sorry, I'm a bit edgy," I explained.

Duck started the car, pulled out into the road and the radio crackled into life.

"Unfortunately, due to the current crisis, we have had to suspend broadcasts from Radio One. Instead, we have some decent music but, before that, a warning from The Government. The warning reads *'Please watch out for ducks and please don't feed them, pet them or look them in the eye. And if you're on the A in Yorkshire1, you may be in trouble as a large swarm or paddle or whatever the collective noun is of ducks is has been seen heading north in what has been called by an expert as a formation'*. In place of the scheduled programme, we now have Terry Wogan with some drizzling wit, amusing banter and ropey songs. This programme was recorded earlier in the century."

We switched the radio off and looked at each other aghast.

"Re-runs of Wogan!" I exclaimed. "We must be in terrible trouble!"

"Never mind that, we need to get north ahead of the ducks or we are all dead," said Duck, putting his foot down hard on the accelerator.

"I wish you'd stop talking about death and we're going to be killed and all of that. And I also wish you'd pass that large lorry with all of those precariously perched orange and green oil drums on it."

"He's in the outside lane," Duck explained.

"So, under-take him," I suggested.

"That could be dangerous and against the Highway Code."

Duck peeped his horn, well the car's horn, but the lorry in front just sped up.

"Flash him," I suggested to which I just got one of Duck's looks. "With the headlights," I added for elucidation.

"This lorry does not want to be over-taken," Duck said.

"And it's speeding. That's almost 90 miles an hour. And those green and orange oil-cans don't look safe to me, look at the straps, they're all rather tenuously joined to the main body of the lorry itself. It's quite dangerous, I feel."

Duck put his foot down in an attempt to catch the lorry and the car shuddered to 80, 90 and then up to100 miles an hour, bouncing us up and down on the uneven road.

"Look," I shouted, "highly flappable it says!"

"Not flappable, flammable, flammable!"

"Oh, that's not good then, is it? Or is that inflammable?"

"They are the same word. Flammable, inflammable, means the same thing."

"Surely not. One means it is flammable one means it isn't."

"No, they both mean the same! It's one of the vagaries of the British language!"

"So, which is which?"

"They are both the same and..." said Duck who was having trouble holding onto the car as we got up to 110 miles per hour "...

mean that they are both likely to burst into flames at any instance. So, we'd better get him out of our way."

"You couldn't close your window, could you, it's getting a bit breezy in here? And he's doing 110 miles per hour now, that really is dangerous with that load."

"Get out of the way stupid truck!" Duck shouted, using his single hand to manually wind up the window, meaning that the car started to veer across the carriageway.

"Erm, actually, that breeze is quite refreshing, no problem, leave it open…"

"Get out of the overtaking lane, you stupid moron!" Duck shouted as we reached the brow of a blind hill in the dual carriageway as the car reached 120 miles per hour. The lorry showed no sign of budging.

"Do you know, when all this is over, I must get to the opticians," I said. "Once upon a time, I used to be able to read a number plate at fifty yards but, now we're only three or four foot off this guy in front and, do you know, I can't make out a number plate at all."

"Hey, that's a good point," Duck agreed.

"And, you know, these eyes are really playing up. I could have sworn I'd just seen a duck on top of those prettily coloured but highly dangerous orange and green drums. Daft what your mind can do, isn't it."

"You are mistaken," scoffed Duck. "There isn't a duck. There are *three* ducks."

"Oh," I said, "glad I was wrong there!"

And we swapped a double take. And screamed.

The ducks were working on the straps which kept the drums precariously on the lorry, trying to cut into them, pulling them, loosening them.

"Erm, Duck," I suggested, latching onto their evil plan, "maybe it would be a good idea to pull over for a while and, well, let them go?"

"Yes, maybe, but there seems to be a little problem with that," he replied.

"What's that?"

"Well, according to my foot here, the brakes have failed."

I looked on in horror as I realized that we had now gone over the brow of the hill and were now on a long, downhill stretch of road that stretched out in front of us.

"Oh, and the steering seems to have gone, too."

I looked fleetingly, desperately towards Duck then back to the bouncing lorry just feet in front of us. The ducks had slackened the oil drums and these now started to bounce almost free of their straps. The ducks were not about to stop. They kept chewing, tugging, tearing away at the straps which were helplessly giving way to their frantic efforts.

"We are dead meat," I suggested as I looked ahead at the sharp incline.

A sliver of the strap tore, slowly.

"Yes," said Duck as he frantically pulled at the wheel with absolutely no effect. We stayed bumper to bumper with the lorry and its lethal load. If this was a film this would be very exciting, though it is less so, it being a book.

The ducks hovered into the air, pulling the straps with them, tugging desperately. With one final tug, the straps flew off and the drums were free of the truck, at last. The ducks, their task complete, swooped up into the air, circled the car, dropped a little memento onto the windscreen and disappeared into the distance, cackling dementedly.

"They knew it was me," said Duck. "They want me dead."

I looked at Duck, maybe for the last time. He had a look of resignation on his face.

The drums in front of us bobbled, wobbled and stopped, ready to fall, finally, on top of our out-of-control car. We were both silent.

As we prepared for our deaths, the lorry in front suddenly veered wildly to the left, into the inside lane. As it did, the drums bobbled for a last time, wobbled a little, then toppled off the lorry to the left of the road, exploding into a huge cloud of orange and black smoke. The lorry, free of its load, careered into the oncoming lay-by, parting with large bang.

I breathed a sigh of relief.

"Phew," I said, "that was close."

Duck looked at me.

"We're safe," I added.

"Yes, you could say that," said Duck, "just small matter of no steering and no brakes to deal with now. Any ideas?"

"Mrs. Merganser! Mrs. Merganser! Mrs. Merganser? Are you there, Mrs. Merganser?" called the policeman from below the terrace of the stone-built houses on the far edge of the small village. "Mrs. Merganser!"

There was no movement from behind the dingy net curtains for some time. The policeman, a young, worried looking man with a fledgling moustache, tapped his feet and wondered what to do. He had been given the task of evacuating the small village, something that had proven to be an easy thing to do until he had come across number Nine Hungry Cat Mews, the home of Mrs. Merganser, according to his printed sheet.

Mrs. Merganser was a well know "difficult" woman in the little village so it was not a surprise to our policeman that she refused to move today.

"Erm, Mrs. Merganser!" he repeated, half heartedly.

At last, out of the corner of the window, there was a small flicker of life. He could just see the top of a purple hatted head.

"What?" came the curt reply from the crack in the window.

"Oh, erm, we're evacuating the village, the ducks and all, you know, and erm, well, we're evacuating the village."

"Good, get on with it then," and the window closed.

"No, no!" shouted the policeman.

The window opened a little again.

"What now?" asked an exasperated Mrs. Merganser.

"Well, that means everyone, includes you too, you see. To be evacuated that is. To safety and the like. If that's okay?"

"Not necessarily."

"But the ducks."

"Yes, the ducks, the ducks, always the ducks. I don't care. They're ducks. Only ducks."

"But the ducks are coming," exhorted the young policeman, realizing that this didn't sound too terrifying in itself.

"Yes well Christmas is coming, young man, but that won't get the place clean and tidy, will it?"

And with that non-sequitor, the window snapped shut.

The policeman could have sworn he'd heard a little chuckle from behind the net curtain but maybe he was wrong, so he shrugged his broad shoulders, realised the futility of it all, climbed back into his mini squad car and drove off into the fields away from the almost totally deserted village to continue his task and growing that moustache.

I awoke bemused in my recollections of what had happened. I was also bemused as to why I was alone and where I was. However, I did not panic, I was too busy shaking to do that and the slight feeling of total paralysis in my entire body was slowing me down too much to actually panic.

My tired eyes did not recognize the surroundings. They were both strange and dark. Very dark. So, where was Duck? Was he still alive? Come to that, was I still alive? Looking around, I realised I was still in the car. The car that was out of control. The car that had lost both its brakes and its steering. And yet... I realized that my bladder was full and that I needed the toilet. Urgently.

I gathered my wits. It did not take long. So, where was I? Locked in a car, somewhere off a main road. Or maybe not. Outside I could hear nothing save for the cold wind whistling round and making me realize that I really did need the toilet, urgently. And I was an open target for the ducks.

The ducks? What had happened to the ducks? Had Duck been attacked by ducks? Was he still alive? I shuddered at the thought. Of him being dead, that is, not at the thought of him being alive. After all, I knew he was our last hope.

Outside, the wind was beating itself into a quiet fury against the invisible trees. Inside, I needed the toilet, urgently. I was letting my darker thoughts grab me, roll me around and show me a locked toilet door. I was in danger of panicking. But I knew that my destiny was in my own hands, that I had to get out of the car and face whatever was out there, as long as I could get to a toilet first.

I gritted my teeth but that didn't help much. So, I pushed against the car door. And fell out of the car and onto my head; it wasn't locked after all.

The wind blew straight up my trouser leg and I knew, just knew that I really did need the toilet.

Here, alone in the outside and totally unprotected world, I felt totally unprotected. Apart from the revolver that Duck had given me. I felt it in my hot, sweaty hand for reassurance. I felt reassured. But I still needed the toilet.

I got up and walked lop-sidedly along, bumping into things, until I had courage enough to open my eyes. When I did, I still saw nothing or nobody (or is that nobody and nothing?) with only the slow, whistling wind disturbing the cold evening air. I hoped there was a toilet nearby. The large poplar trees at both sides of the small lane I found myself on swayed and shook violently and I shivered with cold in the freezing night air.

I walked for what felt like hours and hours but wasn't, as I still hadn't had a chance to have my watch fixed, seeing nobody, hearing nobody, feeling all alone in the world. So, I quickly nipped behind a tree for relief. Normally, people would have passed at this time but, strangely, I was undisturbed.

I knew I was open to attack, so when I was finished, I swiftly zipped up my trousers and marched on, ready to find shelter against the cold night air and the threat of death from the ducks.

Then, behind me, I heard, during a lull in the wind, a quiet, slalloping sound. I stopped but did not dare look around. It stopped. Breathing quietly, I started again. So did the slalloping sound behind me. I stopped, it stopped. I started again, it started again. I began to walk, it kept with me, I speeded up, it speeded up. I ran. It ran. The slalloping noise just kept pace with me. Eerily.

And I realized, with horror, that I must be being tailed by a duck. A killing machine, after its next victim. I did not know what to do, though panic seemed too obvious a choice, so I kept on running with the slalloping sound always keeping pace. I could not throw it off.

I loosened my pace to a slow walk and the noise kept pace. I realized I had to take action. Putting my hand deep into my pocket, I checked on the revolver. Cocking it, I slowly began to pull it out of my pocket, slowing my pace as I did. When I had almost stopped, I span on my heel, eased the revolver from my pocket and fired the gun three times at my foe. As I looked up from the ditch I had fallen into with the kick-back of the shots, I looked out in fear of what I may find.

"What are you up to?" asked a voice from behind me.

"Argh!!" I replied.

Duck looked at me. "It's you!" I exclaimed.

"Yes, that I know but I think you'd do well to keep the noise down, there are ducks around, you know."

"What? Who? Where? How?" I asked.

"Ducks. Have you forgotten? Eating stuff, killing people, havoc wreaking things."

"Yes, I know that! I just shot one!" I screamed.

"Erm, no, you just shot a plastic carrier bag that had attached itself to your shoe and just happened to have a little bit of rain water in, explaining the slalloping sound," Duck explained. "Good shot, though, I think it's dead."

"But it was following me!"

Duck smiled a wan smile.

"It's hard not to do when you're attached to somebody," explained Duck. "Still, you got it and we're safe from it now."

I was going to complain but, as I looked across the road, I noticed a dimly lit house on which was sitting at least a dozen ducks. Duck looked at me, coldly.

"Pity we're not safe from them things up there."

"I've got a revolver!" I screamed, as I was wont to do.

"Yes, with three bullets left in it. Not enough for a dozen or more ducks, I'm afraid. You've done an excellent job of drawing attention to us, with the shooting and all, but if we just stay down here for a while then..."

"We'll be safe?"

"No, we'll just put off the inevitable gruesome death for a short time. We are heavily outnumbered. Makes me so pleased that we escaped certain death by a fluke accident when our car had lost both steering and brake power at one hundred miles per hour. I felt so lucky when that lorry full of mattresses veered in front of the car, slowing us down to manageable speed before I could apply the hand brake and guide us, with my foot, into a lay-by. Seemed quite a charmed life at the time. Was even thinking of doing the lottery when we got back. And then this. Thanks. Good work."

"I don't remember anything of that," I correctly added.

"No, you were unconscious. Passed out, I think."

"So, we're not saved, then?"

"Only if you believe in life after death," Duck added as we looked at the growing number pairs of black, staring eyes on the roof of the house opposite.

"Do you know any good prayers?" he asked.

"No. Well, The Lord Is My…"

"In that case, do what I say. Run like hell!" and with this he leaped up and started to run down the road. Then he stopped and looked at me, still in the ditch.

"You mean now?" I asked.

"Yes, now!" he replied, shoutingly. So I did.

As I did, I could feel a mighty swoop of feathers behind as the ducks, as one, rose into the air, realising that their quarry was suddenly in sight. In the dark night, I ran and ran and ran as I had never run or ran before. Behind me came the drooling beaks of the devil ducks, intent on attack, ready to feast, cackling, calling, almost laughing.

They were gaining on me. I could just see Duck ahead of me but, with water building in my eyes, I could see little yet I could still hear the ducks. My legs started to feel like lead weights but I ran, I ran, I ran and then, to my right, I could make out a small shaft of an electric light. A door had opened, out of nowhere. Through my tearful eyes I glimpsed Duck, leaping and bounding over a garden fence into the safety of the stone-built terrace. I called up one last reserve of energy.

The ducks did the same. I could feel their presence, closer, closer. The sharp smell of death hung in the air. I could smell their murderous down getting closer and closer.

As I reached the fence, I leaped and my foot crashed into the wood, tripping me onto my head and I crashed into a nice border of flowers before rolling along the grass and smashing into a small greenhouse.

"You'll pay for that young man!" shrieked a woman's voice as I felt my collar being lifted and my body being thrown towards a door and the happiest sound I'd ever heard as the door slammed shut.

Unfortunately, it was slammed shut in front of me and not behind me.

I looked up to see a black cloud of ducks suddenly bearing down on me.

I heard their wings like nauseous death descending on me. I smelt the blood. I heard their cackle.

And I passed out.

THIRTEEN

I awoke with a dull thudding pain in my head. At least I awoke. Slowly, cautiously, I opened my eyes to find that, contrary to one of my worst nightmares (that of being eaten alive by ducks, one of the other ones was being beaten to death by babies with rusks), I had not been mauled to death by a pack of blood thirsty ducks (or had the life sucked out of me by two thousand leeches, another one. And not being able to find my car in a car park. That's a recurring one, too).

Indeed, looking blearily about, I seemed to be in one piece, even if my head appeared to have an extra lump where once there wasn't one. I winced as I prodded it.

I did not recognize my surroundings. I had difficulty recalling what I had done recently, what I had said, what had happened to me; it had been traumatic. I normally only found myself in this state after a heavy bout of cider intake but I couldn't recall drinking, so it may have been cider after all. All I could recall was the flapping of a million wings above my head. Then a darkness, a blank. The sound of those wings, the smell of those wings, the sight of those wings were etched in my memory, like a Brueghel painting, hideous yet beautiful in some exhilarating way.

As I tried to focus my eyes, I could see, just, a dimly lit room, dominated by a huge brick fireplace and the dying embers of a welcoming fire. Above the fireplace hung a huge oil painting of a woodland scene where a woman, dressed only in red Wellington boots, was furiously kicking a mallard to death. It was a strangely comforting sight. The trees and the lake were nice, too.

I thought I was dreaming but I knew I wasn't.

The rest of the room was almost indistinguishable in the dark light. I could just make out the dull outline of an armchair, a gold standard lamp and enough curtains to hide three separate elephants under, yes, a well curtained room it was, though there were no elephants, well, none that I could see, though there may have been some behind the curtains.

Or maybe there were none. Or weren't any.

Through the dark, I could smell sulphur. At least, I thought it was sulphur. Raising my head carefully from the settee I now realized I was laying on, I could just about see a door. A bright electric light crept, yellow, around the door edges until the door flung itself open, showering the room I was in with bright, electric light. Before I closed my eyes to the blinding electricity, I just about caught sight of an old woman in Wellington boots. But, before I saw anything else, I had to cover my eyes as then light stabbed into my brain and made it hurt. Hurt a great deal.

"Ouch, the light, the light!" I cried.

"Oh, you're awake, then," said Mrs. Merganser.

"Ow, erm, yes, at least, I think I am," I tentatively replied.

"Your friend's awake!" she bellowed, belying her fragile frame and her age with the noise she made, like a fog horn turned up to eleven.

My head thumped.

"Oh, good, I am so pleased," came Duck's withering reply, laced with a total lack of sincerity.

"Duck?" I ventured.

"You won't catch me with that again, I can tell you," replied Duck, "but, yes, it is."

"Oh, so, you're back from the land of nod," said Mrs. Merganser as she toddled towards a chest of drawers by the fireplace and began to rummage about. "About time, a man of your age."

Only in the light of the door could I see she was old but her grey hairs and her years did not stop her having a distinctly sprightly gait.

"Erm, can I ask where I am?" I asked.

"Yes, you can. Go on then," she responded.

"Where am I?"

"Safe," she replied, obscurely, "at least for now."

Duck appeared in the doorway. He looked at me.

"Must you keep passing out? That's twice today, could be a medical condition, of course..."

"It could be the life threatening positions I keep finding myself in since I met you!" I protested.

"Oh, get you. Youngsters today, don't know what life threatening is, I can tell you. Softies," interjected Mrs. Merganser.

"Yes, well," added Duck, "sorry about having to get ahead of you, you just drew the short straw, I suppose..."

"I don't recall drawing straws!"

"... but I had to survive and if I needed a decoy, you were the perfect one. Oh, and we didn't draw straws, I was speaking hypothetically, of course. Though it's a good idea for the future..."

He smiled, wanly.

"This is Mrs. Merganser, by the way. She's the one who dragged you through the door away from certain death. Say hello and thank you."

"No time for that," Mrs. Merganser said as she toddled briskly around the room before making a graceful and tidy exit through the door.

"But I could have been killed," I said, ruefully.

"You're going to have to stop saying that, the power of positive thinking, self fulfilling prophecy and all of that. And that's only been twice you've been a hair's breath away from certain death today. Get used to it, grow up."

I tried to smile but couldn't. The smile from Duck's face melted and he looked at me in a very menacing way.

"And, anyway, it's not *YOU* they are after, it's *ME*. So don't give me your 'Oh I could have been killed', look, I'm going to be killed one day by these creatures and all just to save this planet. They will kill me, they will get their way and I am ready to die!"

Talk about self fulfilling prophecy...

"You are nothing to them but another meal. But me, me, I'm their big one, their raison d'etre, their, oh, big thing with bells on, they get me and they get the planet. Do you get that?"

He stopped talking but continued to quake uncontrollably.

I did get it. He breathed heavily. And gulped. And stopped shaking. But kept staring.

"It's kind of getting to me. Okay? And when did I last have a crisp? No wonder I'm a wreck. I don't want to die a wreck! Actually, I don't want to die. But if I have to, I'm ready. Unlike you, you great big wet piece of linen masquerading as a human being! Sorry about that last bit but I'm under some pressure here."

I smiled in a kind of yes-I'll-accept-that-don't-worry way.

"But can you just explain the short straw bit again?" I asked.

Before Duck could hit me, there was a stifled though strong explosion from the cellar and through a plume of yellow smoke, Mrs. Merganser appeared, covered in soot and smiling.

"Well," she said, "I reckon that batch is good and ready. Just one small problem."

"What's that?" asked Duck.

"I seem to have lost a wall or two somewhere, so we are somewhat, erm, exposed."

We raced from the ruins of the house straight to the car. The herd (?) of ducks outside was taken by surprise and seemed too astonished to take the opportunity given to them, missing the chance to ambush their adversaries. Indeed, some were more than merely astonished; some had been blown to tiny little pieces by the explosion and many pieces of duck festooned the car, so we needed to employ the windscreen wipers before we set off.

We sat in the car, breathing heavily.

"We were just in time, I think," said Duck, perspiring.

"That's a pochard," said Mrs. Merganser, pointing to a smudge on the windscreen. "I didn't know pochards were involved. That's not right."

I did not take in the full significance of this comment, still suffering, as I was, from shell-shock, a bang on my head, partial blindness and Duck's tirade. And his driving. This had got even worse, maybe due to tension, maybe due to the blood seeping down from his head from the explosion, maybe because he was just plain mad. And my head kept banging on the roof of the car. And it hurt.

"There's more than pochards," Duck said, emotionless in the response to Mrs. Merganser's comment, "I have seen scaups, tufteds, eiders, goldeneyes, shovelers, teals, grebes, gadwalls…. you name them, I've seen them."

"Smews?" asked Mrs. Merganser.

"Oh, yes."

"That *IS* bad. Very bad. It's very bad smews."

There was a pained silence. Not surprising.

We bumped and banged along in the car into the night at a frightening speed. I did not know where we were going but was getting used to this by now. Duck kept saying we were headed for "our ultimate destination" which was fine by me as I still had a headache and my feet were also a little bit sore. I asked him to explain the role of our little grey haired passenger.

"Mrs. Merganser is the saviour of the world," he told me.

"Another saviour? Isn't that three today?" I asked.

There was a tap on my shoulder. It was Mrs. Merganser.

"Don't you go listening to all he says to you. I may be the saviour of the world but, on the other hand, I've four fingers and a thumb. I will only be the saviour of the world if I save the world."

I couldn't argue wit that. "And will you?"

"Well, I'm pretty naffed off at these ducks running the country, I must say. The corner shop was closed last night and they have to take the blame for that! And to think I voted New Labour. Anyway, so annoyed was I at this duck thing that I decided to find their Achilles heel. And I did."

"See, there is an atmosphere about her," said Duck.

Smelt like sulphur to me.

"Achilles heel?" I asked.

"Yes, a little bit of research does wonders," she added.

"In Knaresborough library you can find out a great deal about ducks. In fact, I was a little surprised to find that there is a single huge section just on ducks alone in there. It's bigger than the crime section, though not as big as cookery and martial arts. Which kind of worried me. Anyway, if you ask the library attendant, Bob, he can tell you all and he did, directing me to the works of the great Sir Darrington Womersley, who had pointed out many years before of the Third Equinox when the ducks would come and claim this planet for their own. So, I borrowed all of the books and, when I went back to renew them, Bob had gone. Duck related incident, they said. The ducks knew he was onto them, I reckon. So, being heartless killers, they got rid of him. Cruel and heartless. The ducks, that is, not the library staff. Bob actually was quite nice, though he had a dodgy moustache. The ducks found my address through the records of the library. So, now they are after me. But I am not worried as I know of their Achilles heel."

There was silence for a short while.

"And that is?" I asked.

"Well, Sir Darrington chronicled his feverish efforts to thwart the Second Equinox's coming but, luckily it didn't happen. The ducks just forgot about it or something or maybe they got distracted by satellite television. Anyway, it didn't happen. He knew it would resurface some day and the information was still of use as it really didn't have a sell-by date. It's as relevant today as it was when Sir Darrington was around. Which is only eight years ago, by the way. His predictions and his answer to the only way to deal with the ducks have come to the fore this time. Their Achilles heel is known and can be used."

"And their Achilles..."

"So, the information, the knowledge is in the library, as are the answers to all of our problems should we care to take a careful look.

From health problems to the nature of chemical engineering to ducks, it's all there. Of course, we won't all have a Bob to direct us to the truth but the truth is there should we decide to search it out."

"Okay, so libraries are good, but, so, their Achilles…"

"We now know. And we will be able to use it."

"And that is?"

"What? Their Achilles heel?"

"Yes. It is?"

"You want to know?"

"Yes!"

"Oh."

And there was a silence.

"Well, their Achilles heel is… they don't like being blown up. Hence the smell of sulphur and the huge bombs we have in the boot of the car."

As Duck bounced the car into another pot hole, I wondered about my own safety. But we now had their Achilles heel: they didn't like being killed.

"Once the ducks were happy waddling, eating soggy crusts of bread, but they now crave for world domination. Well, must get boring just pootling up and down a river all day. I suppose world domination actually gives you a meaning in life, doesn't it? But the world is what they are after now. And they're doing a good job of it, by all reports. And they won't stop. These are not sane logical creatures. They are ducks driven by a higher force. They have driven out the nicer ducks and now only these devil ducks exist. We need to find the source of their evil and destroy it. Only then may we see the return of the rather pleasant and occasionally comic little creatures we used to know and love. And if we don't, well, it's the end of the world as we know it. And I don't feel fine, thank you."

"We're almost there," said Duck as we pulled into the large floodlit abbey.

"This is their place. It has mystical meaning. It was mentioned in the Koran, the Bible, Gibbons Rise and Fall of the Roman Empire, certain editions of The Highway Code, the 1623 Folio of some of Shakespeare's plays and in foreign versions of the Da Vinci Code. The latter was a printing error, of course. The actual location ties in with their apparent fascination with time and their natural inability to read a watch face. This was foretold in the early editions of the Bible. Here you go," added Mrs. Merganser, passing me a book.

"This is The Reader's Digest Guide To Birds Of The British Isles," I corrected her.

"Yes, well, it comes in useful for knowing which is which. But here is what I meant to give you."

And she handed me the following pieces of paper torn from Sir Darrington Womersley's prophetic book.

The Mandarin duck. Found in China and Japan on ponds and streams. They feed on green water-plants and people. The Mandarin duck is a perching duck. It likes to perch on trees. And dive on people from great heights.

Mallards are vicious sorts. The drake is the one with the green colored head and big teeth while the female is the one in brown with a gun, sometimes. It is thought to be the ancestor of our farm ducks, just a lot less friendly. They eat small insects, snails and plants in ponds and streams and often kill people just for the fun of it.

Gadwall. Often confused with the mallard, despite the different spelling, this is a regular visitor to places where humans gather. The Gadwall can be found both inland and in coastal areas from mid September onwards. Give them a wide berth, they'll pull you apart as soon as look at you.

Pintail. Sounds nice but deadly. The pintail is a prized trophy with the cock bird being particularly sought after because of his striking plumage and many methods of killing men. Beat it to the punch, as the saying goes. Many small waterways and lakes in Ireland are visited each winter by flocks of pintail, which explains the large number of deaths there that have always gone unexplained. They use their head as a weapon.

Eider. Large marine duck of the genus Somateria, family Anatidae, order Anseriformes with a side order of bread. They are found on the northern coasts of the Atlantic and Pacific oceans. The common eider is highly valued for its soft down, which is used in quilts and cushions for warmth, mostly after death. The adult male has a black cap and belly and a green nape, often with a small cape that hides a knife. The rest of the plumage is red and white with a pink breast and throat, while the female is a mottled brown with bloody bits. The bill is large and flattened and both bill and feet are olive green and ready to do damage to human flesh.

The Tufted Duck, or the "tufty" as it is referred to inexplicably, as it bears no resemblance to a squirrel, is both a migratory species and a killer of the first order.   The large freshwater lakes are the regular haunts of tufted ducks, especially during the latter part of the season when local numbers are swelled by migrants who come for mass slaughter. They decoy well and, when feeding on freshwater, can be extremely good at distracting your attention whilst one of their mates takes you from behind.
The Widgeon has been described as the killer of killers. It has white flash of the speculum on the wing, the whistle of the duck and its fast flight make it one of the most dangerous species on the foreshore. Numbers of wigeon over-wintering in these isles has led to many winter deaths as they get really blood thirsty in the colder months.

Shelduck or Duck Tadorna Tadorna of family Anatidae. Posh name, killer all the same. It has a dark-green head and red bill, with the rest of the plumage strikingly marked in black, white, and red chestnut. The drake is about 24 in long. Widely distributed in Europe and Asia, it lays

10–12 white eggs in rabbit burrows on sandy coasts, and sometimes plants bombs in holiday homes; can be seen on estuary mudflats, hunting men. Takes pride in what it does.

Teal. Any of various small, short-necked, argumentative, dabbling ducks of the genus Anas, order Anseriformes. The male is dusky grey with blood stains; its tail feathers ashy grey; the crown of its head deep cinnamon or just knife shaped; its eye is surrounded by a nasty black band, the sign of the seasoned assassin, glossed with green or purple, which unites on the nape; its wing markings are black and black; and its bill is black though often spattered with red for obvious reasons. The female is mottled brown but still likes a good kill. The total length is about 14 in but like all things small, very good in a scrap.

Shoveler. Fresh-water duck that can also kill on land. Anas clypeata, family Anatidae, order Anseriformes with potatoes, so named after its long and broad flattened beak used for filtering out small organisms from sand and mud or slipping into peoples ears. The male has a green head, white and brown body plumage, black and white wings, grey bill, orange feet, and can grow up to 20 in long though some have been recorded at twenty seven feet. The female is speckled brown and normally very annoyed due to PMT. Spending the summer in northern Europe or North America, it winters further south to kill more humans.

The Ruddy. So called because it is a ruddy good killer. The male has a brilliant blue bill, made for the kill. It also has a long and stiff tail, good for getting you when you least expect it.. During Spring and Summer, the feathers are colorful to attract females for breeding and to confuse people so they can get a good shot at them. The Ruddy belongs to the "Stiff-Tail" species which kills for the sheer enjoyment (see also Manx Shearwater).

The Bing Bong Duck. Also known as knob-billed ducks because of its fatty comb on top of its bill and not due to its masculinity. The bill is black in memory of those it has killed. We don't think this duck really exists but we like its name.

Smew, a small white bird, buttocks bright grey, thick pointed bill with saw like edges that can cut through a man's flesh in no time. The most horrible killer duck in the range, hates humans, smiles as it kills, brown teeth, two black eyes that see into eternity. If you see one, run like hell. Often the subject of bad puns, for example, "That's bad smews" and "That's the end of the smews".

The Pochard. Another of our killer diving ducks that can murder under water, the pochard or "poker head" as it is generally referred to by people, is common on the bigger waterways and lakes where it likes to drag down its human quarry and drown them to death. The local breeding population is augmented by a large influx of migratory killing birds at the end of November when the training of killer squads can be very productive. Rafts of these duck congregate on the open expanses of water in ready to do battle with their mortal enemy, the human being. One day they shall rise up and the Third Equinox will bring the end of the world order...

"Well, they pretty much all sound the same to me," added Duck. "Killers, all of them."

I turned the pieces of paper over, looking for something more, some sparkling insight.

"Is that it?" I asked. "Just a list of ducks? No explanation of their killing, no reason for this destruction, no insight?"

Mrs. Merganser looked at me.

"You people, always looking for meaning, reason, depth, something hidden, you just don't get it. No, there is no reason. Well, there is a reason: they are just nasty little pieces of work. You see, you guys can look for in-depth, hidden, clever, smart explanations all you want but, the truth is, life is usually an awful lot simpler than we'd hope it is. Nature is just nature and you can't muck about with it. The truth is simple, they're just evil little things who like to kill. Though that's a hard one to swallow, I suppose. You lot like to have more complex explanations: they've been hard done by, they had bad upbringing, they were abused, they came from broken marriages, they didn't have shoes, boo-hoo. There must be a *reason* to their badness. Well, I'd like to give you a complex labyrinth of meaning but, to be honest, there isn't one. There is no reason, no reason at all to explain this, which is scary enough in itself. If there was a reason, this would make us feel more comfortable but, no. They just like blood and they the taste of human blood. Oh, and the occasional crust of bread..."

Yes, it was hard to swallow.

And all the more terrifying for its starkness.

The car stopped. We were at an abbey which I could just about make out through the darkening gloom. The trees around the abbey swayed in the wind.

This was their lair.

Mrs. Merganser and Duck leaped from the car, oblivious to the danger or the small group of ducks circling in the night sky.

"There is a small group of ducks circling us in the night sky," I pointed out.

"Yes. I know, they are of no concern to me. We have our job and we must do it. Mrs. Merganser, the explosives, if you may," said Duck.

Mrs. Merganser opened the boot of the car and together they carefully lifted out the bombs.

"Right, well, since you don't need me, I'll go and see if I can find a toilet," I said as nonchalantly as possible.

"Toilet? Oh, no. We need you to build a raft," Duck said.

"A raft?"

"Yes, one of those floating things. Put it on water and, hey presto, you don't drown. Know what I mean? Now get on with it, we don't have much time here. Have you not noticed the small group of ducks circling us in the night sky?"

"Yes, I pointed that out and...right," I said. "A raft. A raft? Why do we need a raft?"

"Well," explained Mrs. Merganser, "the ducks are not in the abbey here itself, they are in a cavern, close by. A cavern that can only be reached by the small river that runs by the side of the abbey. There, we think, sits the Mother Duck, at the end of the cavern, surrounded by her acolytes, all desperate to defend her, willing to give up their life to protect her, even when faced with human beings who are, of course, their sworn enemies. So, we need to get to her. Get her, we end the threat. And she's at the end of the small river that runs into the cavern. As we don't fancy paddling, we need a raft."

"Yes, but..."

"This just may give us the element of surprise. We don't think that they'll think that we'll think to attack that way so we may just fool them. Of course, they may be onto us and kill us in a slow and painful manner before we get to them but that's the risk we face in trying to save the world."

"Was that a two man raft then?" I asked, hopefully. "I can mind the car and..."

"No, a three man raft. We need you, too," Duck intoned.

"Oh, good, glad I'll be involved directly," I lied as I went off to organize a raft. As you do.

Fifteen minutes later, we all stood on a raft.

"Nice work," said Duck, rather surprised. "Can't be easy building a raft at night with no real preparation. Impressive. Stout work with the ropes there, too."

"Actually," I pointed out, "I'd like to take the credit but there just happened to be one at the side of the river there. Quite fortunate, really. Just where those ducks had been..."

Duck and Mrs. Merganser looked at me and each other.

"Where the ducks had been? Maybe this is a set up. Still, it's do or die time," Duck said.

"You sure you don't want me to wait here and mind the car? I don't mind, really," I asked.

"Too late," said Mrs. Merganser as she spied a small number of ducks swimming towards us. "Quick, the bread!"

We all carefully grabbed the small bread rolls Mrs. Merganser had made and tossed them towards the four or five ducks that approached us. As they welcomed their gift, quacking hungrily on the crusts, we all ducked down as the small detonators within did their job and the ducks were splattered into the night air.

"Quick, row or punt or whatever it is you do on a raft!" cried Mrs. Merganser. "Let's get going, they were only the advanced guard and the worst, I feel, is yet to come!"

And she was right.

The noise of the explosion had raised the alarm in the headquarters of the ducks. Through the smoke and gloom I could just make out a rippling movement. Here they came.

Duck, now realizing that it was time for the culmination of the ducks' reign of terror, knowing that it was a now-or-never moment, punted or rowed us manically forward.

"Be ready, boys, prepare yourself," said Mrs. Merganser, menacingly, "for they are undoubtedly ready for us."

"They must protect their leader and will let nobody harm him or her or it!" shouted Duck through the smoke and mist. "But we must prevail! We must kill their leader, break the spell or be subservient to these ducks... forever!"

It was quite dramatic.

The idea of being subservient to a duck was abhorrent to me. I felt a churning in my stomach, followed by a lurching on our vessel as Mrs. Merganser toppled into the water and three ducks appeared at the far end of the raft.

Duck swung around, peering desperately into the gloom as the three ducks started to pull at the ropes which held the raft together. From nowhere, five further feathery ducks appeared, swimming in formation, circling the bubbling area where Mrs. Merganser had disappeared. Her head and shoulders appeared, momentarily.

"Go on, go on, don't wait for me!" she screamed through the bubbles. "Our destiny is in your hands! Kill them pesky little beasts! Kill them before they kill you! Oh, I wish I'd taken those martial art swimming lessons at the local baths!!!"

And with that the five ducks dived onto her head and pulled her, struggling, under the water.

"Hit the ducks!" I yelled but Duck could not move.

I picked up a handful of bread and tossed it to the three ducks at the rear of the raft. They could not resist their natural inclinations and bit into the bread, exploding as they did, the force of the explosion sending the raft scuttling madly and uncontrollably towards the torch-lit cavern, cutting a swathe through the mass of guard ducks at the mouth of the cavern. The remaining bread catapulted from the raft as we sped along, inadvertently feeding the ducks, causing more explosions as
the blood-thirsty hoards instinctively fought over the food which was proving so deadly to them.

In a matter of seconds, we were floating, just, in the lair of the ducks on what remained of our raft.

Shell-shocked and coughing through the smoke and feathers, we held onto the rafts remnants as it floated quietly through the dead duck bodies towards the purple glowing cavern of the mother duck. Looking up, I could see no threat now from the ducks which had terrorised and paralysed our nation so quickly and efficiently. Only carcasses were left now, floating dead on the water and bobbing up and down against the shallow banks on either side. All that seemed to be left was one huge, black figure of a duck that slept, regally, at the other end of the cavern. And we were getting closer and closer.

"Duck!" I cried but there was only a groan in reply.

Duck was lying in a heap on the raft, his one arm dangling lifelessly in the water.

"Oh, no!" I said to myself as I saw a gaping wound in his head caused by the dismembered bill of a duck which had exploded just seconds before. At the very moment of triumph, it looked as though Duck was to die. A tear fell from my eye. Then his face turned to mine.

"It's up to you now, don't give in, the battle is almost won but, my friend, the war isn't yet over...."

Dying and he comes up with a cliché like that. Class.

"You must kill the mother duck. If she lives, they will be back. If she dies, they will never return. You must kill the mother duck. Kill her and you save us all. If she survives, we will never be safe."

"But, look, they are all dead."

"Oi, cloth ears, listen to me. You need to kill her. Okay? Here," he said, controlling his rage, "take this," and he thrust a French Stick (or baton as I think they are sometimes called) into my hand. "I saved this... for *her*."

And with that, his head clunked to the floor of the raft. The air was still. I held his stick in my hand, looked down and whispered in his ear, "This one's for you, Duck."

The mother duck's head slowly moved as it heard me talk. Its neck began to stretch up, one huge threatening black eye opening and its down ruffled in an intimidating manner. It was a truly terrifying sight.

"...and don't balls this up," said Duck, with his last words. Which was unfortunate, as I already thought he was dead. And the shock of him speaking made me jump and drop the bread into the water. I'd ballsed up.

"Heck!" I mouthed but Duck didn't hear this. "Now what do I do?"

The big black eye first looked at me, then at the large plasma screen with BBC News on it and then back at me. I looked at Duck, motionless on the raft. The mother duck raised her wing, slowly. I gulped. From under the wing of the mother duck emerged four large ducks, as big as large dogs, their down blood red, their eyes deep black and angry. I stood rigid, the hair on the back of my neck standing on end. I was cornered, unarmed and slightly worried.

The four ducks, with one last gasp of air, opened their gleaming orange bills to exhibit a white set of shining fangs, glistening in the dark torchlight. They looked to their mother for guidance, eyeing me as their prey.

The command was slow and noisy. The mother's bill yawned open again. It clamped shut again with a resounding clack. I missed a breath as the four ducks moved, gliding into the water, headed towards me. I started to pray.

The ducks moved towards the raft but their instinct made them stop. One had seen something in the water. It went over, carefully collected it and went back to the mother, signaling for the other three to follow. They dropped their offering at the feet of the mother. She quacked, thankfully and lent over.

They had given her the French stick (or baton).

Instinctively, she leant over and hungrily bit into the bread.

I was knocked off my feet as the explosive in it blew the mother's head clean off and into the air, taking the other four ducks with her into oblivion.

I covered my eyes and looked up to see the dying carcass surrounded by the dismembered bodies of her four duck guards, blood and feathers everywhere. And then the large plasma screen slowly toppled onto the small, dead group. As it fell, the station changed from BBC News to the "Buy This Now, You Moron, Shopping Channel" which, as it toppled, was ironically advertising Duck Protection Materials at knock down prices.

How ironic. Their natural instinct and modern technology had been the death of them. Sir Darrington Womersley was probably right. Though I never really knew what he was on about. Suffice to say that the mother duck was now dead and were safe. According to Duck. Dead Duck.

I needed to get away. I didn't look, didn't stop to check that they were dead, just paddled and paddled what was left of the raft out of the cavern, me and Duck's body. To safety, I hoped.

But didn't dream.

EPILOGUE

I buried Duck in a quiet ceremony at the pretty church that overlooked the river close to his home in a tailored coffin. I thought it was fitting. Few people came, well, nobody but me, but I knew the significance of his actions and his bravery and his untimely death. The sun shone hazily in the sky.

Maybe summer would now come?

Brushing away a small tear, I bade my last respects and trundled through the gravestones, wanting to get back home to safety, normality and a comfortable pair of slippers.

My nightmare was over. Duck had sacrificed his life to save a country that did not realize, did not care, about the plight it had been in. The Government put it all down to "opposition spin" and denied that the ducks had been a threat to public safety, despite over six million casualties. The Chinese take-aways had special deals on Crispy Duck in Pancake Rolls.

Somewhere in the country, people were taking soggy crusty crusts in old bags to lakesides and feeding the ducks again; somewhere, the summer sun was finally breaking through the dark threatening clouds. Somewhere, there were bluebirds and meadows and singing cows.

I tried to forget all that had happened, all that I had seen, but I knew that those searing images would be difficult to erase. Maybe I would have them in my mind's eye forever. Or maybe it'll be all gone by next Sunday. You never know, the mind's a funny thing.

I told myself the nightmare was over.

I read from the book I'd found on the raft, dropped as she fell from it to her death by Mrs. Merganser.

"The ducks shall rise up three times and they shall kill, maim and do other nasty things to human beings if allowed to. The natural order will be upended and we shall be in thrall to the ducks. Until we

find a saviour. A saviour in the shape of a one armed man who shall come from nowhere to save us and shall give up of his life in so saving us. Find that man and we find salvation. Oh, and a woman with plastic legs and an oblivious man. And recall, beware the ducks for ducks are dangerous. Blow them up."

How prophetic.

Walking back close to the river where it had all started just over one hundred and seventy pages or so ago, I heard a small fracas. Through the quiet afternoon sun, I quaked as I saw a solitary duck flapping wildly towards me.

"No," I thought, "not again, not a recurring nightmare!"

And then, behind it, came the baying, howling, barking noises of four loping Labradors, just like my beloved dog which I had lost some days before, though different. They bounded after the duck and, catching it, began to unmercifully pull it slowly apart. When its body stopped twitching, they looked up into the fading sun, their cold breath hanging around their fangs in the late afternoon air.

I looked on in anguished horror as they returned my stare.

As one, they looked at each other, winked, wagged their tails high in the air and started to lope towards me, baying and howling.

My nightmare was about to begin again.

Now I got it.

So, I ran. I ran like hell. Before they got me.

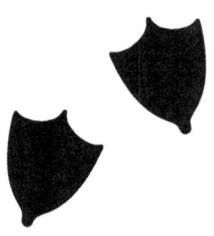

Two beans, a bean and a half, half a bean and a bean, by the way.
The answer to the question earlier.
In case you were wondering.

The author (who is me but I like this pretentious approach) used to be in selling, has been employed as a trainer for too many years and now has to work for a living. He never wanted to work but found it paid more than writing for a living, which he still doesn't do.

He's got a degree in English but a fat lot of good that turned out to be.

Anyway, the author (this is SO pretentious!) has been writing for years yet has never had anything published, performed on television or radio, or filmed, partly because he's never tried it out and thought he was too old to do so. Okay, so some people know him from radio but that is reflected glory and doesn't carry a salary of significance.

He has two kids, a wife and a large mortgage and still thinks he can play football at his age, though he doesn't. Golf's a better bet now.

His favourite film is still Duck Soup.

Not many ducks were harmed in the making of this book.

Thanks for reading it.

len.horridge@btinternet.com

What may have been already been said about THE DUCKS...

"Douglas Adams meets the Marx Brothers[1]," Adrian Boulton

"Have read the front and back covers plus page 1, made me laugh so might even give pages 2 and 3 a bash at some point... it is worth buying and it doesn't take up much space on the bookshelf and he's not going to stop sending us these emails until you all do." Donna Mackenzie

"A masterly debut from the pen (computer keyboard?) of Len 'Horrible' Horridge, a leading member for many years now of the team of unpaid scriptwriters for the "Wake Guptar Wogan" wireless show. Len is consistently funny, although I suspect some or all of this particular work may have been undertaken during an "altered state of consciousness. Highly recommended." Jonathan Havard

"I chuckled three times on the first two pages" David Hopps

"Keeps my table from wobbling," a waitress at The Beehive in Thorner

"Is there a Victim Support Unit?" Iain Crump

"I'll never get back that three hours of my life," Alan C. Jones

"Well, I haven't enjoyed myself in bed so much for a long time! It's all there, the fear, suspense, mounting trepidation....and then there are the laugh out loud funny bits (big bits mind, not just yer average). Caution: You will never look at a duck in quite the same way again." Janet Heather Middler

---

[*]*He never did, by the way. But he did write brilliant books*

Len Horridge